Already Published

A Friedman Lecture Fund Monograph

PLANNING RULES AND URBAN ECONOMIC PERFORMANCE
The Case of Hong Kong

The Hong Kong Centre for Economic Research

The Centre was set up as a research and educational trust under a trust deed signed in 1987. It supports research and publishes studies on public policy issues to promote understanding of economic affairs and provide alternative policy choices.

The Centre's work is assisted by an international board of advisers:

The Centre is an approved tax-exempted charitable trust controlled by Trustees and financed by sales of publications and voluntary contributions from individuals, organizations and companies.

Director: Richard Y. C. Wong

The Hong Kong Centre for Economic Research
School of Economics and Finance
The University of Hong Kong
Pokfulam Road, Hong Kong
Tel: (852) 5478313 Fax: (852) 5486319

A Friedman Lecture Fund Monograph

Planning Rules and Urban Economic Performance
The Case of Hong Kong

Samuel R. Staley

Published for

The Hong Kong Centre for Economic Research

by

The Chinese University Press

ISBN 962-201-632-4

THE CHINESE UNIVERSITY PRESS
The Chinese University of Hong Kong
Sha Tin, N.T., HONG KONG

Printed in Hong Kong by Regal Printing Ltd.

The Friedman Lecture Fund was established from proceeds obtained from a public lecture given by Dr. Milton Friedman on 24 September 1988 in Hong Kong. The purpose of the Fund is to support research that leads to an improved understanding of the role of markets in economic life. To this end the Fund supports the work of individual scholars and institutions. The Fund is operated jointly by the Hong Kong Centre for Economic Research and the School of Economics and Finance of the University of Hong Kong.

Contents

LIST OF TABLES

LIST OF FIGURES

Foreword

The HKCER Paperbacks are planned to be studies of medium length in which economists would analyze a policy issue from an economic perspective. Authors are invited, in particular, to consider the circumstances which encouraged or inhibited the translation of ideas into policy.

The post-war economic growth of Hong Kong has been hailed as one of the miracles in the annals of economic development. For both residents and visitors the most striking and visible feature of this miracle is the breathtaking pace of change in Hong Kong's skyline as skyscrapers rise proudly and compete for attention. The achievements of Hong Kong in urban and land development outshine not only North American and European urban centres, but also the fast growing cities in East Asia. Rapid urban and land development in Hong Kong has occurred amidst the challenge of a formidable physical terrain, limited supply of land, and massive waves of immigrants that have streamed into the territory over the past decades.

To a large measure the enormous success of urban and land development in Hong Kong is a consequence of a "pro-market" planning and development process, which has allowed developers to operate in an environment of reduced uncertainty. This has lowered the cost of land and urban development and have contributed to lowering prices for residential, industrial and commercial premises from what they otherwise would have been. This has made it possible not only for Hong Kong to develop land and property, but to support economic growth and development.

This study by Samuel Staley points out the important tensions and conflicts between contemporary planning systems and urban economic development that exist in the West. These planning systems disrupt market-based decisions by politicizing the land development process and stifle urban growth. In the longer run economic activities simply moved elsewhere leading eventually to both urban and economic decline. The success of urban and land development in Hong Kong during the post-war period is due primarily to an urban planning system that facilitates and encourages growth by protecting private property rights and ensuring economic markets work smoothly and efficiently. Staley reveals and explains the contractual basis of the Hong Kong system and its functioning. He goes on to argue that the Hong Kong system has much to offer as a model for other countries.

The Hong Kong system, however, will be compromised as a result of the recommendations proposed by the Hong Kong government in its *Comprehensive Review of the Town Planning Ordinance*. According to Staley these proposals will severely affect the process of development planning. The changes will be economically disruptive because they increase uncertainty in property markets, weaken the contractual nature of land development, and provide more opportunities for planners and the general public to delay development. The result will be more volatile property markets, reduced supply and higher prices and rents.

Staley's arguments are cohesive, insightful and enormously practical. He puts forward a set of practical recommendations as to how the disruption of property markets can be minimized and efficiency of the planning process preserved. Following several decades of rapid growth and development, urban re-development has become a major concern of Hong Kong. The problem is being further exacerbated by the transformation of the economy from manufacturing to services as a consequence of the opening of China. The change has given rise to new demands in the pattern of land use.

The central message of this study is that clearly delineated private property rights reduces economic uncertainty and are essential for development to take place. The issues discussed are not only relevant for land development and town planning issues in Hong Kong, they have important lessons to offer on how to prevent urban decay and help cities to flourish. China too can learn from Hong Kong's experience as she struggles to pursue urban re-development after decades of stagnation.

The Trustees, Advisers and Directors of the Hong Kong Centre for Economic Research must formally dissociate themselves from the conclusions of the Paperback, while welcoming its timely contribution to a major issue in Hong Kong.

Richard Y. C. Wong
December 1993

The Author

Samuel Staley teaches urban and regional economics at Wright State University in Dayton, Ohio, USA and is Vice President for Research at Buckeye Center for Public Policy Solutions, an independent public policy research organization also based in Dayton. Since 1987, he has been an economic development consultant, working with local governments as well as university-based research centres.

Mr. Staley has authored or co-authored over two dozen studies, reports and articles on urban development issues and policy, spanning a wide variety of topics including enterprise zones, inner-city revitalization, mass transportation, property rights and economic development, and zoning. He is the author of *Drug Policy and the Decline of American Cities* (New Brunswick, N.J.: Transaction Books, 1992), a book on the devastating consequences of the drug trade on central city economies. His work has appeared in a variety of publications including the *Journal of Urban Affairs*, *Economic Affairs*, and the *Wall Street Journal*.

Mr. Staley is also the author of *Planning, Uncertainty and Economic Development in Hong Kong: A Critical Evaluation of the Comprehensive Review of the Town Planning Ordinance* published by the Hong Kong Centre for Economic Research in October 1992 as well as a chapter on housing and land (co-authored with Richard Y. C. Wong) in *The Other Hong Kong Report 1992*.

Acknowledgements

Writing this monograph was an extremely complex and challenging task and could not have been undertaken without the generous support of the Hong Kong Centre for Economic Research (HKCER). The HKCER funded several trips to Hong Kong and coordinated extensive interviews with people knowledgeable in planning and economic development. Y. C. Richard Wong, the Centre's director, provided valuable insights into the problems facing Hong Kong's economy and the role of the planning system in providing an environment for economic growth. Richard also demonstrated much appreciated patience by giving me ample opportunity to revise and rewrite the manuscript.

Invaluable contributions were made by dozens of individuals who interrupted their frantic schedules to ensure my understanding of Hong Kong's planning system was adequate and complete. While many will not agree with the conclusions, the study is immeasurably better as a result of their input. Although space does not permit acknowledgement for every one involved, I would like to specifically thank the following for providing much needed perspective and data: A. G. Eason, R. D. Pope, Bosco C. K. Fung, Peter K. W. Fong, M. Y. Wan, John Greenwood, Lyall Alexander-Webber, Anthony Walker, Trevor Farnworth, Andrew Bliss, David Faulkner, Anna O. N. Sze, Richard Bates, and two anonymous referees whose comments and suggestions were most helpful. While some errors undoubtedly remain in the analysis, despite the best efforts of all those involved, the responsibility lies solely with the author. Eliza Chan of the HKCER provided extremely important administrative support, without which the project could not have been completed as efficiently or effectively.

Finally, I would like to thank Alex Chafuen and Carl Helstrom of the Atlas Economic Research Foundation in the USA for alerting me to the HKCER's work.

Executive Summary

This monograph analyzes the relationship between town planning and urban economic development, using Hong Kong as a case study. The *Comprehensive Review of the Town Planning Ordinance* published by the Hong Kong government in 1992, proposes several important reforms to the town planning system in Hong Kong that will have a significant impact on Hong Kong property markets and economy. The reforms will be economically disruptive because they increase uncertainty in property markets, weaken the contractual nature of land development, and provide more opportunities for planners and the general public to delay development.

The proposals highlight important tensions and conflicts between planning systems and urban economic development. The current planning system in Hong Kong facilitates and encourages growth by protecting private property rights and ensuring economic markets work smoothly and efficiently. In contrast many modern planning systems disrupt market-based decisions by politicizing the land development process through planning. The Hong Kong case provides an excellent opportunity to assess the relationship between town planning and economic development and analyze the implications for planning reform in Hong Kong as well as other countries.

The Hong Kong property market is the focal point of the territory's recent growth, accounting for 45% of the capitalization in the Hong Kong stock market, 60% of Hong Kong's investment expenditures and almost 40% of bank lending. Loans made by licensed banks for property development and residential purchases increased 545% from 1981 to 1991. Property markets have contributed as much as 40% of total government revenues during the 1980s, varying from 60% of all government revenues in 1980 to 27% in 1986. As Hong Kong's economy develops into a global financial and services hub, smoothly functioning commercial and residential property markets will be pivotal.

The experiences of other countries, particularly the United States and the United Kingdom, are used to provide an important context for assessing the theory and practice of contemporary planning. Recent experiences in these countries suggest that attempts to promote efficient land development will be disappointing because planning is fundamentally incapable of harnessing the information necessary to coordinate complex decisions over land use and resource allocation. In fact, smoothly functioning land markets are more capable of ensuring privately and socially beneficial land use allocations.

While the proposed system attempts to minimize delays introduced into the development application process through statutory guidelines and limitations, the experience of other countries suggests that delays will be much greater than the statutory time limit or the expectations of public officials. Thus, at a minimum, developers can expect delays of between three months and one year, depending on the complexity of the development and the degree of opposition by the public. The current proposals fail to provide guidelines concerning the appropriateness of objections or which parties are permitted to raise objections.

The most disruptive element of the planning reforms proposed in Hong Kong will be the introduction of a random component in the land development process. The delays will be difficult to calculate since developers will be unable to predict the response by the public or local planners to proposed developments. The new system also represents a significant departure from the existing system of development control and land-use regulation, adopting more comprehensive planning rules similar to those found in advanced industrialized countries. These reforms will infuse even more uncertainty into the development process as new formal and informal rules are created. Many developers believe the new system of land-use planning and regulation represents a shift in philosophy among government officials to a more interventionist role, particularly in light of the events surrounding the Mid-levels on Hong Kong Island and Tsuen Wan. Moreover, developers will likely tolerate non-statutory delays to the plan application process since they will want to preserve a cordial working relationship with the existing planning authority. The new planning system will thus create a substantial amount of uncertainty with respect to the timing of potential delays, adding to swings in the building cycle and variation of property prices.

The potential impact of delays in land development are then analyzed using case studies of projects in Hong Kong. If development were delayed for one year, added costs per project on Hong Kong Island could range from HK$241 million for a 500,000 square foot commercial office building to HK$603 million for a 1 million square foot office building, depending on prevailing interest rates. If all new office space added on Hong Kong Island in 1991 were subject to a one year delay, the added costs for financing new developments would exceed HK$1 billion. A one year delay could add between HK$480 per square foot to HK$603 per square foot to the cost of commercial development, depending on prevailing interest rates. Similarly, a one-year delay in the construction of new residential units could add HK$1.1 billion to the cost of developing a 5 million square foot residential estate. Overall, the added costs to residential construction could vary from HK$250 per square foot to HK$300 per square foot, depending on prevailing interest rates.

The Hong Kong case also provides a unique opportunity to study the regulatory burden of planning on land development. Changing plot ratios in the Mid-levels, for example, could have imposed an economic burden of HK$28 billion in lower property values by reducing the developable residential floor area by 38%. Planners imposed significant costs on industrial developers in Tsuen Wan by reducing plot ratios, although precise estimates of the burden imposed by land-use restrictions were unavailable. Nevertheless, the analysis of the Mid-levels case study revealed that the regulatory burden imposed by the *Comprehensive Review* could be significantly more than simply delays in development.

One of the most salient weaknesses of contemporary planning is its failure to recognize property rights which are essential for ensuring economic development. Recent attempts by planners to impose restrictions on land development have weakened the underlying property rights framework and contractual nature of development in Hong Kong. To the extent planning decisions contribute further to the erosion of property rights, the economic impacts could be important as developers slow the pace of land development in commercial, industrial, and residential areas causing prices and rents to rise further. The key issue of compensation and betterment were inadequately addressed in the *Comprehensive Review*. An increase in discretionary regulatory powers in the land development process without a parallel commitment to making compensation for the economic impact of adverse decisions will compromise the stability and certainty in property markets. In essence, government is released from any obligation to calculate the costs of its decisions. An important instrument of accountability would be destroyed. Thus, preserving the existing contractual nature of development by adopting a system of compensation that protects property rights in development is essential for ensuring a dynamic, efficient property market in Hong Kong.

The study also found that the potential impact on delays in the plan application process on government revenues could be significant. The uncertainties introduced into the planning process will reduce the value of leases, a major source of revenue for the government, and actual delays in the development process could easily generate losses in the tens of millions of dollars for specific projects through losses in general rates, profits taxes, and stamp duties. Two case studies of existing projects revealed that losses to the government in terms of permanent and temporarily foregone revenues could be substantial. For example a 800,000 square foot commercial and residential unit could imply government revenue losses of $10.3–18.7 million, a similar 350,000 square foot unit could cause losses amounting to $7.1–8.5 million.

To minimize the disruption of property markets and maintain the stability and efficiency of the existing planning process, the study suggests the following recommendations:

1. *Design a development application process that avoids un-necessary delays by implementing a system where plan applications are automatically approved* unless the Town Planning Board rejects

the application. This would shift the presumption of planning process in favour of development and provide incentives for the planning board to avoid unnecessary delays in processing applications.

2. *Clearly define the scope and interest of objections to planning applications* by limiting objections to parties directly affected by the proposed development and "bad neighbours".

3. *Limit objections to the plan making process.*

4. *Adopt a system of compensation that preserves the contractual nature of property development in Hong Kong,* anchored to a clear recognition of property rights and the economic costs imposed by regulation.

5. *Subject planning decisions to an economic impact analysis* to ensure the full impact of planning and regulatory decisions are revealed before reforms to the system are adopted.

6. *Eliminate the planning certificate procedure* to avoid unnecessary delays in the plan application process.

CHAPTER 1

Planning Rules and Economic Growth:
An Overview

A property developer stands in the middle of several hundred acres of empty fields in the heartland of the United States. Although there is a gentle roll to the land, it lies only one kilometer (about half a mile) off of a major highway connecting over five million people within ninety minutes. The spot seems ideal for a major American-style shopping complex, complete with sprawling one or two-storey buildings and ample surface parking.

The developer proceeds to hire the architects and consultants needed to design and develop the complex. At this point, he is only a speculator, purchasing land from local farmers at a premium with the expectation of earning larger revenues from the commercial development. The local "bedroom" community of about 30,000 people requires that any new land under development be approved by local zoning and planning authorities after the developer submits the proposal as part of a "Planned Unit Development" (PUD).[1] The local zoning and planning regulations also require that the city council, consisting of seven members elected by the community, approve the plan.

Being aware that planning a new commercial development is often a long and tedious process, the developer has retained planning consultants to begin working with local planning authorities at an early stage. By the time the PUD is submitted to the local planners, all

---

1. PUDs are used to control large developments that involve a variety of uses and building types.

the details will have been worked out, including the number of entrances, traffic lights, water and sewer systems, densities, public accesses, and types of businesses allowed in the new complex. By the time the PUD is submitted, the developer has already invested hundreds of thousands and perhaps even millions of United States dollars in the speculative project. After months of negotiation, revision, and compromise, the PUD is accepted in principle by the city's planners and is ready for submission to the local planning board.

Despite the lengthy period of land acquisition and design, the formal plan approval process has not even begun. The project must still be approved by the Local Planning Board (LPB) and the City Council. The first signs of political difficulty emerge as the developer submits his plans for approval to the planning board, composed of local residents appointed by members of the city council (who are elected at large). A local anti-growth group objects to the new development, arguing that the project will disrupt the bedroom community's cozy, semi-rural environment. Although the anti-growth group was started by a cluster of residents living near the proposed development, the movement quickly gains support from local and regional special interest groups, such as environmental coalitions, community preservationists, and traditionalists. The anti-growth group begins a stalling process, using formal and informal methods to pressure the city council, and the planning board to delay approval of the PUD. A survey is commissioned by the city council to determine the community's view on new development. The results reveal that a majority of the community favours development, feeling that added jobs, more convenient services and higher tax revenues offset the potential threat to their quality of life.

Finally, after the developer and local officials have invested more than two years in planning and negotiations, the city council overrides the objections of the no-growth community group and approves the project. Unfortunately, the national economy is now in a recession. As businesses default on loans, regional banks are less inclined to invest in real estate developments because of the speculative nature of such developments. Thus, the line of credit originally extended to the developer is no longer available. Over the next six to nine months, the developer works with the banks, slowly persuading them that the project is financially sound given its location and lack of other retail opportunities in the immediate area. As the national economy begins to emerge from the recession, the banks renew their commitment to the project and the equipment rolls in to begin construction. The project will take another year to be completed, although the developer has already obtained commitments from three major regional and national retailers to anchor the new development. Thus, it is almost five years after the process of land development began that the project might finally become a reality.

This example is representative of the problems and delays inherent in a decentralized, politically controlled land development process. While the example is taken from the United States, similar problems can be observed in planning systems in countries as culturally different from the United States as the United Kingdom, the Netherlands, and Australia. More important, similar delays and uncertainties may become institutionalized in Hong Kong if current proposals to reform planning and zoning laws are adopted, seriously compromising the territory's ability to adjust and adapt to world economic conditions.

While the United States system of town planning is litigious and unique in many respects, the delays and uncertainties surrounding land development result from the system's open, cumbersome public process, not a peculiar political culture. The example used to open this study did not include numerous other mechanisms available in the United States system that delay development projects even further, such as law suits challenging the impact of the development on the community and environment or subjecting the project's approval to a community-wide referendum (ballot-box zoning). In other words, the example illustrates the system as part of the normal land development process.

Local Planning in Hong Kong

The potential impact of a similar system in Hong Kong can be illustrated by modifying the illustration only slightly. Currently, developments go through two approval processes in Hong Kong. The first requires developers to submit their plans to the Buildings and Lands Department to ensure the development meets important design and construction standards to guarantee public health and safety. The proposed development must have adequate water and sewer, electrical wiring, material support for the building, etc. If the development meets these design and safety criteria, it is approved, often within thirty days.

A second approval process is required if the development includes certain types of uses that may be considered incompatible with existing or neighbouring uses.[2] In this case, the developer must submit a planning application that will be reviewed by the Town Planning Board consisting of seven members appointed by the Governor. While the board may be compared to a Board of Zoning Appeals in the United States, most projects are approved relatively quickly, within 90 days of submitting the application. Moreover, most development plans are approved routinely.

Most Hong Kong planners and some politicians want to open the current development process to more public scrutiny in both the planning and development application processes. These changes could delay the development of residential and commercial projects by two to nine months. In an economy where major developments are completed in two years, these "reforms" could add as much as 40% to the time required for development. More important, these delays will be unpredictable. The nature of the objection and approval process is sufficiently vague that developers will have few ways to predict whether the project will be delayed for two months, nine months, or over a year. In an economy where banks expect repayment of development loans in three to four years, the risks and uncertainties surrounding property-related loans will force interest rates up, crowding out investment and increasing the cost of new developments.

The result will be higher costs and, ultimately, prices for all

---

2. These are also called "Column Two" uses are explained in more detail in Chapter 4.

consumers: businesses will pay higher prices for office space and residents will pay higher prices and rents for flats. To the extent demand for commercial and residential space remains high, prices will be pushed upward as fewer residential and commercial flats are developed. In an era where middle-income residents in Hong Kong are being squeezed by higher rents for private flats, and politicians are increasingly hearing calls for middle-income housing subsidies, delays in the planning process have important political and social implications (See also Wong and Staley, 1992).

Although the potential costs of town planning rules can be significant, particularly in tight land markets such as Hong Kong, proponents of planning have used a wide range of arguments to support their calls for an increasingly sophisticated planning system on the local level. While a more complete discussion of planning is reserved for Chapters 2–4, a brief discussion of the purpose of town planning provides an important context for understanding arguments for more extensive planning controls in Hong Kong. Indeed, as the next two chapters illustrate, much of the current argument for planning controls mirrors debates in more advanced industrialized countries such as the United Kingdom and the United States.

The Planning Perspective

Town planners attempt to improve the quality of life of urban residents by ensuring that resources are used most efficiently (see Stollman, 1979). Planning, in its most general form, simply involves making decisions about how resources will be used to achieve some future goal (see also Bristow, 1984, pp. 2–4). In this context, virtually everyone plans.

But town planning, and land-use planning in particular, has a more specific purpose than simply allocating resources to achieve an agreed upon goal. Planners are not merely facilitators in land development, and the effects of their decisions are not neutral (Bristow, 1984, pp. 5–6). Whether reinforcing existing patterns of land use or actively intervening in land development and conversion, the planners have an important role in the *process* of land development. Of course, whether the planners' role is active or passive has significant implications for the pace and pattern of economic growth.

In the past, Hong Kong planners have found their role to be somewhat of a passive one. Increasingly, however, Hong Kong planners are following the examples of planners in other countries by becoming more interventionist and active in manipulating land development. The implications will be significant, not only for the quality of life for Hong Kong residents, but also for the prospects for sustained economic development within the territory.

At the heart of modern town planning is a deep suspicion of the ability of economic markets to allocate resources to the most socially beneficial use. Most land development, according to many planners, is based on "speculation", divorced from the long-term consequences of development on the local community. Economic decisions are not integrated or comprehensive, sacrificing non-economic considerations such as aesthetics, urban design, infrastructure, urban amenities, or the appropriateness of land-uses for the sake of the "bottom line". Urban planners Arthur Gallion and Simon Eisner argue, for example, that this form of economic speculation contributes in large measure to building a city, but the speculator assumes no responsibility because he is not concerned with the use of the improvement. That responsibility and the obligation for maintaining it are shifted to others when he transfers ownership. The motive of speculation consequently induces inferior quality; he is concerned only with the least possible initial cost and the greatest possible profit (1986, pp. 222–23).

In principle, town planning allows communities to rise up and override the narrow, speculative economic interests of property owners and private developers by regulating urban development and land-uses. Unlike private developers and landlords, planners trained to act in the public interest will consider quality of life issues that might be overlooked in the flurry of land speculation and development.

Theoretically, planners supplant market allocations of land-use determined by prices in real estate markets with more "rational" and "socially beneficial" allocations determined by a process of town planning. Market allocations of land, according to standard planning theory (and application), tend to be "haphazard" and "disorderly", lacking any underlying rationale other than satisfying the selfishness of the land owner. A farmer, for example, will only consider how much a developer offers him for his land, not the impact of the new development on his neighbours or community. Without planning, cement factories can locate in residential areas, steel foundries can operate in the basement of apartment buildings, or restaurants can be set up in commercial office buildings. Town planning and its associated tools can avoid these "incompatible" uses by requiring that the "right" development occurs in the "right" place and at the "right" time.

The application of planning principles has taken on different characteristics in different places, depending on the specific nature of communities, nations, cultures and political systems. This is particularly true in the case of Hong Kong, as this study will show. Nevertheless, despite the variety of land-use planning systems, important lessons can be learned from the diverse experiences of other countries, particularly since the Hong Kong planning system appears to be in a significant state of flux. Attempts to evaluate the impacts of proposed changes to Hong Kong's system may be aided significantly by looking at countries as their planning systems have developed.

Planning Rules and Economic Development

Town planning is one of the more obscure functions of government, but it has far-reaching implications for the everyday lives of local residents. The local planning system often defines the "rules of the game" for developers and has a direct impact on the quality of life and economic health of local communities, whether they operate in an industrialized, service or high technology economy. Urban economist Harold Hochman has argued that development regulations are "critical to the well-being of the urban economy" (1988, p. 102). Planning rules and procedures impact how quickly local economies adjust to new challenges, such as the rising importance of financial services or the move towards information based manufacturing technologies. Poorly designed planning systems hamper a community's ability to marshal resources effectively and productively. Indeed, Hochman warns, "excessive or inappropriate intervention in development in land use ... can prove crippling, because it impinges directly on location, the engine of the urban economy" (ibid.). An economy tangled in a web of planning and zoning rules may find its ability to adapt to new realities compromised. In modern economies driven by international economic and political events, cumbersome, time consuming planning systems with unpredictable delays can directly reduce their competitiveness.

Ironically, despite its pervasive presence in the lives of local residents, town planning's impact on economic development and the pace of change in cities has been largely ignored. Even in Hong Kong, where many observers have long acknowledged the importance of relatively fluid institutions in economic development, the role of the land-use planning system is glossed over. In a recent analysis of industrial change in Hong Kong, for example, economist Yin-ping Ho acknowledges that a "very stable yet flexible institutional framework" including "an efficient and well-disciplined" government, a "relatively non-arbitrary legal system", commitment to free trade, and the widespread use of English as the language of trade and finance was an essential component of Hong Kong's success (1992, p. 27). The efficient and stable system of land-use planning that allows for market determined land uses, however, is left outside the purview of Ho's study of Hong Kong's structural economic change.

Ho's oversight is common and understandable. Planners typically view their position and responsibilities independently of their impact on economic development. Issues concerning employment, economic growth, and economic adjustment are the province of economists, business interests, and economic development specialists. The planner's role, in contrast, is merely to guide development in the most appropriate and socially beneficial direction to enhance the quality of urban life.

Similarly, economic development specialists and policy analysts have tended to focus on issues that directly impact a company's bottom line. Regulatory interventions into markets for land-use often have intangible impacts and are difficult to quantify. As a result, scholars and policy-makers have focused on policies that directly impact the decisions of corporations, such as tax policy, rules over business ownership, financial disclosure, employee benefits, etc., meanwhile slighting the crucial role of the property market in greasing the wheels of the economy.

The public is often left out of the planning/development loop entirely, even though they are the ones most directly and significantly impacted by land development and economic growth. Jobs lost to a neighbouring city, province or country through cumbersome planning processes directly reduces the economic vitality of the local economy and may reduce long-term prospects for growth. In the fast paced economy of Hong Kong, if the construction of a new housing estate is delayed through the town planning process, the effect on housing prices can be significant, further compounding existing inflationary pressures. New industrial and commercial development may also find that a streamlined planning system emerging in Guangzhou or Singapore may be preferable to the uncertainties and vagaries of a more open planning system in Hong Kong.

The Purpose and Plan of the Book

Unfortunately, the economic impacts of town planning have not been addressed thoroughly in the Hong Kong context. This study will attempt to fill this void by analyzing more thoroughly the impacts of town planning on the economic vitality and development potential of an urban economy. Chapter 2 provides an overview of the role and purpose of town planning and its relationship to the Hong Kong economy. This chapter describes the conceptual context of town planning, its purpose, and a critical appraisal of planning from an economic perspective.

Chapters 3 and 4 analyze the attempt to apply local and regional planning systems in the United States, the United Kingdom, and Hong Kong. The United States experience with local planning has important implications for town planning in other countries, particularly Hong Kong, as it moves toward a more open political system. The United Kingdom system provides an alternative model of town planning that is more consistent with the legal and political foundations of the Hong Kong system. Both the United Kingdom and United States systems, however, fail to incorporate a realistic understanding of land development as a market process, and thus the systems create inefficiencies in resource allocation and contributing to inflationary pressures in property markets. Yet, the system that has emerged in Hong Kong, while rooted in the system developed in the United Kingdom, is unique and provides a range of complimentary institutions that favour economic development that are largely absent in the United States and United Kingdom. Chapter 5 provides a detailed discussion of the current Hong Kong planning system and the important role the *Comprehensive Review of the Town Planning Ordinance* (the Consultative Document) has played in planning reforms. Chapter Five provides an analysis and critique of the reforms suggested in the *Comprehensive Review*. The impact of the reforms on property markets and development will be discussed, while also providing a general analysis of the impact of town planning decisions on economic growth and development.

Chapter 6 describes the estimated impacts of delays on property development in Hong Kong, while Chapter 7 more fully discusses the impact of regulatory planning decisions on the economy. This chapter will also deal with the essential role compensation plays in ensuring a stable legal framework in which development is encouraged and protected.

Chapter 8 concludes this study with a summary of the analysis, its implications, and recommendations for improving the efficiency and effectiveness of Hong Kong's town planning system within the context of economic development.

CHAPTER 2

Town Planning and Economic Growth

A general introduction to the origins and intent of town planning is necessary before the full implications of planning or economic development can be discussed. This chapter will explore the intent and purpose of town planning as it has developed in the United States, Europe and Hong Kong, thus laying the groundwork for evaluating the experience of town planning in the United States and United Kingdom as well as looking at reforms proposed by Hong Kong planners in the *Comprehensive Review* released in March 1992.

Hong Kong planners have proposed to substantially revise the current planning system such that it would adopt features common to planning systems in most other advanced industrialized countries. The justification for these changes will be discussed within the context of Hong Kong's rapid economic growth in recent decades. Indeed, as the discussion below suggests, many of the town planning reforms proposed in the Consultative Document are consistent with broader trends toward diverse political representation and a more activist government within the territory.

A more thorough discussion of the practice of planning in the United States and the United Kingdom is reserved for Chapter 3. The second part of the analysis, contained in Chapter 4, dissects the foundations of modern planning theory further and contrasts it with an economic perspective of land development. The role of planning will be critically evaluated within the context of the needs of Hong Kong and its potential for sustained development in a post-industrial global economy.

Origins of Local Planning and Zoning

In principle, town planning attempts to control and manage economic development for the benefit of the general public. Historically, planning in one form or another has existed in every civilization. As cities grew, for example, governments became increasingly responsible for providing basic infrastructure. Planners helped determine the pattern of economic development by their choices of the location of roads, bridges, or, in more modern times, sewer systems. The procedures for controlling land-use vary significantly, depending on the historical development and background of individual countries and communities, but the theoretical concepts and goals are surprisingly consistent wherever town planning is practiced.

The twentieth century, however, marked a dramatic change in the focus and purpose of town planning. Before 1800, most planning was dictated by large economic trends through relatively unfettered markets. Economic considerations determined where textile mills would locate, and cities emerged around an industrial urban core. This spatial arrangement facilitated easy access to factories by workers. This pattern of land use is still evident in old manufacturing towns in North America and Europe. To some extent, it exists in Hong Kong in old industrial districts in Tsuen Wan and Kwun Tong. Residential housing developed around factories producing toys, clothing, and electronics as well as godowns and other warehousing facilities near the port. More recently, residential housing has followed a less deterministic pattern as transportation networks have improved and the economy has shifted toward more flexible commercial and service-oriented economic functions.

In the colonial United States (before 1776), many cities were planned using grid transportation networks with interconnecting streets at right angles. This allowed major roads (avenues and boulevards) to carry heavier traffic fed by secondary road ways (Gerckens, 1979). In fact, this system of transportation planning was pioneered by the canals developed in Venice during the European Renaissance (Mumford, 1961).

Early planning, subsumed by economic concerns, led to significant problems in urban areas according to conventional planning history. High population densities led to public health hazards, shoddy housing, environmental pollution, and congestion, contributing to a general deterioration in the quality of life.[1] Israel Stollman claims that as a result of an economic philosophy of laissez-faire, weak municipal governments, and an agrarian bias in public policy, "some of the worst housing and living conditions experienced by modern man were created in America" during its industrial revolution (1979, p. 27).

As a result of apparent degradation of urban amenities, threats to public health, and potential hazards of rapidly developing urban populations, the first systematic attempts to control the urban environment began in the late nineteenth century in Western Europe and the United States. Many of the early restrictions on development focused on building codes and safety regulations, requiring builders to use certain materials and construction techniques. In Hong Kong, for example, concerns over shoddy construction of tenement housing on Hong Kong Island in the late nineteenth century stimulated the first widespread attempts to regulate the construction and building industry (Bristow, 1984). The potential for fires and concern about poor sanitation prompted public officials to impose controls over building height, site coverage and construction materials.

This pattern is evident in most industrialized countries. In England and the Netherlands, for example, contemporary planning law is rooted in legislation governing housing development (Thomas, et al., 1983). The *Public Health Act of 1875* led to the first public interventions in housing in England, followed by the *Town Planning and Housing Act of 1909*. In the Netherlands, the *Housing Act of 1901* provides the basis for contemporary planning.

---

1. Importantly, this version of urban history and economic development has been largely discredited by economic historians. Modern analyses of the industrial revolution in Europe and the United States balance earlier criticisms by emphasizing general improvements in public health (evidenced by falling death rates and infant mortality), widespread availability of essential commodities such as shoes and clothing, more diverse and healthy diets and rising real incomes. See the discussions in Hayek (1956) and Rosenberg and Birdzell (1987).

Thus, if left to private interests, property development conflicts with broader public interests and degrades the quality of life. For example, without proper planning and land-use controls, town planners argue, mixed industrial and residential uses will erode the quality of urban life as cement factories and other noxious uses pollute the air surrounding schools and recreation areas. In the Consultative Document, Hong Kong planners point to numerous uses they consider incompatible or inappropriate, such as auto repair shops on the ground floors of apartment buildings or textile factories next to temporary housing.

In economic theory, attempts to control for the impacts of the unintended consequences of market activity are called "externalities".[2] In principle, if property rights are not defined well in private markets to the ensure costs (or benefits) of market transactions are minimized, uninvolved third parties might bear some of the costs and receive few (or none) of the benefits. If a plastics factory dumps industrial waste into Tolo Harbor, for example, fishermen may find their livelihood threatened as fish are poisoned. If fishermen cannot use the legal system to provide compensation (presumably from the factory) for their loss, the lost income from the pollution is a negative externality.

A planner might argue within the context of town planning and zoning that the economic and political influence of a major land developer prevents local residents from being fully compensated for the costs of redevelopment. If the developer builds a commercial office building in the middle of a residential block, residents will experience an increase in noise and congestion related to a large number of people moving in and out of the office building. Local residents with diffused interests and little skill in organizing effectively against wealthy property interests would have few alternatives

---

2. The concept of externality has a long tradition in economic analysis. For pioneering work, see Coase (1960), Buchanan and Stubblebine (1962), and Dahlman (1979). For an extensive discussion and application to Hong Kong in the context of environmental policy, see Kwong (1991).

except to move or accept the new development. By deciding whether the project will be approved, the town planner serves as both a mediator and final arbiter over land development, minimizing externalities in the process.

In the attempt to control nuisances or externalities, land-use regulations have expanded far beyond the narrow public health and safety concerns prevalent at the beginning of the twentieth century. As urban populations grow and cities become denser, development begins to spill over into rural and semi-rural areas (suburbanization), increasing pressure to limit and control economic growth. Indeed, one of the primary benefits of the New Towns programme in Hong Kong was to enable planners to more appropriately channel economic development to reduce congestion and decentralize the territory's population and job base (Bristow, 1989). Rather than allowing private developers to "randomly" develop the New Territories, the New Towns would enable the government to manage the growth of Hong Kong.[3]

In the United States, as in other countries, municipalities moved to restrict local growth through a regulatory device called "zoning". Zoning separates land uses according to their function and is usually applied to existing uses (Hollander, *et al.*, 1988). Commercial uses are separated from residential uses, which in turn are separated from industrial uses, under the assumption that intermingling uses detracts from the quality of life of the city. Zoning is now the most common tool used by local planners to regulate land use and development in the United States (Babcock, 1979; Kelly, 1988). Indeed, over 98% of all municipalities in the United States are covered by zoning laws even though federal law does not require it.[4]

Zoning, as a legitimate function of local government, derives its legal authority from different areas, depending on the nature of the

---

3. Unfortunately, as Chapter 4 discusses, the success of the New Towns has been limited in achieving planning goals.
4. Houston, Texas is the only major city in the United States without comprehensive zoning laws. Even Houston, however, has recently adopted very limited forms of land use restrictions such as set-back requirements, site coverage, etc.

legal system. In the United States, for example, zoning was legitimized after the United States Supreme Court ruled that zoning was a legitimate extension of the "police" powers inherent in local self-government. Under United States law, all governments are given powers to protect the general welfare, and land-use regulation (as well as town planning more generally) has increasingly been recognized as a governmental tool for protection of the public interest from narrowly defined private interests. In Europe, however, zoning and town planning legislation grew out of statute. While planning law in England is still bound by common law, comprehensive town planning is an integrated part of national policy.

While modern town planning originally emerged as a tool for avoiding nuisances, it now does far more than simply protect its residents from the external impacts of land development. While early zoning laws and land-use regulations were attempts to control for the spillover effects (externalities) associated with development, modern planning attempts to anticipate development and mandate quality standards in communities. Modern planning is often referred to as "positive" planning where the local government takes a pro-active approach to land development.

The modern general plan considers a number of issues and problems that were ignored by more narrowly defined zoning regulations, and even by the master plans of the mid-twentieth century. The modern general plan guides the physical development of the community, sets long-range goals, and explicitly outlines the desires of the community — including the "preferred" quantity, location and rate of growth — and suggests how those desires will be achieved (Hollander, *et al.*, 1988, pp. 60–1). The modern general plan is also used as an important guiding document for public and private agencies.

Thus, building codes that govern health and safety features in new construction have given way to new codes and standards that govern quality of life characteristics. Typically, there are *building codes* and *planning codes* that reflect differences in emphasis in the development process. Building codes address direct health and safety considerations and are often specific, detailing the types of materials that can be used in construction, minimum sizes (and types) of beams permitted to be used depending on the buildings's size, minimum sizes for electrical wiring, types of insulation, strength of pipes, etc. Planning codes reflect non-safety considerations that effect amenities and quality of life such as the minimum number of rooms, minimum number of electrical outlets, site coverage, minimum lot sizes, and, increasingly, height restrictions.[5]

The Purpose of Town Planning

Town planning, in practice, circumvents market processes in urban development. Decisions about the pace, pattern and nature of urban development and land use are determined by politicians, planners or other appointed public servants instead of by market processes that rely on the price system to coordinate resource allocation. In the United States, for example, zoning boards (elected or appointed) determine whether development will be allowed to occur. In Europe, professional planners are appointed to determine the appropriateness of land development in specific areas. In England, these professionals are given substantial latitude while in other European countries, such as the Netherlands, planning decisions are more rigid (Thomas, *et al.*, 1983). Even in Hong Kong, where the planning system is far less rigid and more open to market-driven changes, a Town Planning Board is appointed by the Governor to make decisions on the appropriateness of new development projects and approve comprehensive plans. Some of these plans are very specific, and are geared toward specific areas such as the Mid-levels, North Point, or Sha Tin. Other plans,

---

5. In the past, height restrictions were imposed because of technological limitations on construction. This is increasingly irrelevant as building technology has enabled the safe construction of buildings hundreds of stories high. Thus, Hong Kong sees taller and taller buildings (residential and commercial) built in popular areas such as the Mid-levels. Height restrictions exist in Kowloon and Tsim Sha Tsui, but these reflect safety concerns for the public in close proximity to Kai Tak Airport. These restrictions have been recently lifted in response to improvements in navigation technology.

such as district plans or Metroplan, are more comprehensive, outlining development paths for future decades.

The *practice* of contemporary planning is fundamentally an anti-market process. Modern town planning attempts to specify land-uses narrowly, leaving little to the vagaries of property markets and the wishes of entrepreneurs. Indeed, market-based allocations of land are considered contrary to the public purpose and are over-ridden by professional planners in virtually every country with a sophisticated planning system. In fact, according to standard planning theory, town planners are considered more capable of determining the appropriate uses of land and resources because of their training and expertise.

Actually succeeding at narrowly specifying land use is not an easy task, however. Planning authorities in all countries have attempted to direct and guide land development through three principals tools: development plans, zoning and development control. Development plans — sometimes referred to as general plans, master plans, or comprehensive plans — are intended to map out future development in socially beneficial ways and maintain an adequate quality of life. Because development plans are the product of a process that includes experts trained to look beyond the narrow interests of private parties, development plans are supposed to represent community interests rather than private interests. The development plan is used as the basis for "guiding" development in socially beneficial directions.[6]

Development control is one of the principle tools used to implement the development plan. Development controls, like building and planning codes, can be separated broadly into two different types: building controls and planning controls. Building controls are used to ensure minimum standards are set in construction or development to protect the health and safety of residents as well as the public welfare. These regulations will specify requirements such as access to running

---

6. Whether this is true or not is problematic. Few planning processes require significant citizen participation or that changes to general plans be subjected to voter approval. In most cases, the social benefits of planning are assumed.

water, bathroom facilities, electrical outlets, etc. If the project conforms to the necessary building codes, permission is usually granted to continue with the development.

Planning controls, in contrast, are used to enforce planning rules developed by local, regional, or national town planners. Planning controls ensure that land is used for its designated purpose (e.g., commercial, industrial, residential, etc.), meets basic design criteria, conforms to neighbouring uses, adheres to the style and architecture of the neighbourhood, and so on. Planning controls are directed primarily toward ensuring that the quality of life of the local neighbourhood is maintained or improved, according to the standards set forth in the planning regulations and the development plan.

The presumption of most local planning ordinances is to disallow any use of land inconsistent with the development plan created by local and regional planning agencies. Ironically, the nature of the public interest, and the way in which town planners are expected to determine the public interest, is often ignored in textbooks on town planning. In many cases, planning courses and texts simply begin by assuming that town planners and their development plans reflect the public interest. In fact, few planning systems, except very decentralized and fragmented one such as system used in the United States, provide formal mechanisms for public participation that are binding. In an overwhelming number of cases, public participation is limited to public forums, or "hearings", on proposed development plans and projects. These forums typically suffer from selection bias since, in many cases, the people affected negatively by an action are the ones that tend to be the most vocal. While community attitude surveys are becoming standard tools for discerning preferences for development, their use is selective and general. Public participation in most countries (including Hong Kong) occurs only at the discretion of the local planners.

Structural Economic Change in Hong Kong

Before developing a more detailed conceptual framework in which planning, its use in other countries, and its relevance to the Hong

Kong economy can be assessed, an overview of some of the more important economic changes and challenges faced by Hong Kong is necessary. Hong Kong has experienced tremendous economic growth and change since the 1950s, and these changes will serve as a critical back drop for evaluating the relevance, significance and potential impacts of town planning on Hong Kong in later chapters. More importantly, as the next chapters show, similar experiences with economic growth have served as the primary justification for planning in the United States and United Kingdom. Unfortunately, the implementation of these systems have served more to hinder adjustment and adaptation in these economies than facilitate it.

One of the more stunning achievements of Hong Kong since the end of World War II and the Japanese occupation has been its increased economic activity and income. Figure 2.1 illustrates the steady rise in Gross Domestic Product (GDP) measured in 1980 constant dollars since 1966 (Hong Kong Census and Statistics Department, 1991b, Table 1b). The Hong Kong economy has increased at a relatively

Figure 2.1: Growth in Annual GDP in 1980 Prices, 1966–92

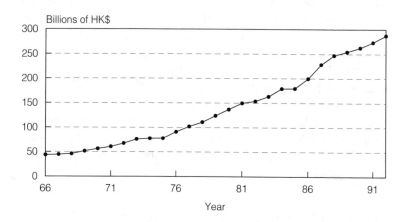

Source: Hong Kong Census and Statistics Department.

steady rate over the past 25 years. This economic growth has lifted the bulk of Hong Kong's population out of the impoverishment common in less industrialized countries in Asia as well as the rest of the world.

In fact, a comparison of Hong Kong's per capita GDP in 1988 with similar data for other industrialized countries demonstrates this achievement. Its growth has also allowed Hong Kong, along with the other "Little Dragons," to challenge the wealth and prosperity of Western industrialized countries (Liu, 1992, pp. 1–7). Data on per capita income reveal that Hong Kong's per capita income of US$14,283 in 1991 compares favourably to per capita income levels of US$17,745 in the United Kingdom, US$20,166 in Italy, and US$20,972 in France (Fig. 2.2). While still substantially below income levels of the United States (US$22,468), West Germany (US$24,553), and Japan (US$27,005), per capita income in Hong Kong has surpassed levels of Spain, Ireland, and New Zealand,

Figure 2.2: Per Capita Income in Hong Kong and Selected Countries, 1991

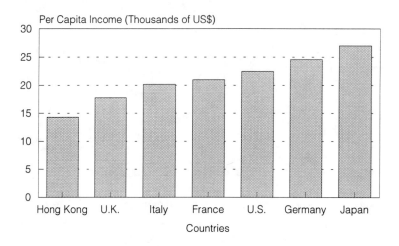

Sources: International Financial Statistics, IMF
Hong Kong Census and Statistics Department.

countries classified as high income economies by the World Bank.[7]
While Germany, the United States, and Japan still outperform Hong
Kong in income, Hong Kong's economy has consistently performed
robustly, and the gap in between the income of Hong Kong's citizens
and those of wealthier countries is closing quickly. Hong Kong, notes
economist Ying-ping Ho, "is now the second most materially com-
fortable place in Asia, second only to Japan" (1992, p. 13).

While overall income and growth trends are upward, the
economy has been volatile during Hong Kong's ascendance into the
class of high-income economies (Fig. 2.3). While GDP growth (in
real 1980 dollars) increased at rates approaching or exceeding 10% in
most years, the Hong Kong economy experienced low levels of
growth in 1967–68, 1974–75, 1982–83, 1985 and 1989–90. World-
wide recessions contributed to slower growth in the mid-1970s and

Figure 2.3: Percent Change in Annual GDP in 1980 Prices,
            1966–90

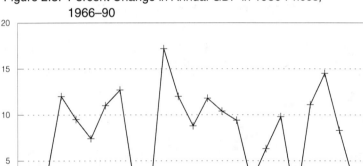

Source: Hong Kong Census and Statistics Department.

---

7. This is the World Banks classification of economics throughout the world. For a
   more complete discussion of Hong Kong's position in this hierarchy, see Ho (1992,
   pp. 13–14).

early 1980s, but political events — the Sino-British negotiations over Hong Kong's future and the Tiananmen Square incident — were partly responsible for sharp drops in growth rates in 1985 and 1989–90.

Note also that Hong Kong's per capita GDP (after adjusting for inflation) declined during the world recession of the mid-1970s, falling 1.1% in 1974 and 1.5% in 1975 (Hong Kong Census and Statistics Department, 1991b, Table 2b).

Per capita GDP growth recovered after 1975, increasing even during the recessions of the early 1980s (although at a slower pace): Real GDP per capita increased 1.1% in 1982, and 4.7% in 1983. This resilience may have reflected the benefits the Hong Kong economy was deriving from economic reforms in China during the 1980s, which opened new opportunities for trade with the industrialized world. During this period China grew to be Hong Kong's second largest trading partner (Ho, 1991).

Real GDP growth fell again by 0.9% in 1985 (the year after the Sino-British Joint Declaration), partly due to the economic slow down caused by the strengthening of the US Dollar (to which the HK Dollar was linked), before increasing 9.6% in 1986 and 12.9% in 1987. Quarterly GDP and real per capita GDP growth levelled off somewhat in 1989, reflecting the uncertainty following the Tiananmen Square incident. Nevertheless, the growth in GDP per capita in constant (1980) dollars was substantial, increasing to $45,031 in 1990 from only $14,236 in 1970, at an annualized rate of 5.75%.[8]

The underlying reasons for this spectacular growth and economic progress have been a source of discussion and research as scholars throughout the world have studied the "Little Dragons". In Hong Kong's case, the influx of migrants from mainland China in the late 1940s and early 1950s was clearly instrumental in providing a supply of entrepreneurs and an eager labour force (Sung, 1991a). In fact, the lack of in-migration from China in the 1980s (since China implemented its reforms) and the subsequent labour shortage has been

---

8. All values are expressed in Hong Kong dollars unless otherwise noted.

suggested as the principal cause of slow growth in the late 1980s and early 1990s (Lam and Liu, 1991).

Investment in light manufacturing was also a key ingredient in the colony's stunning economic progress. Therefore, Hong Kong has been linked to Singapore, Taiwan, South Korea and Japan as an example of how exports of domestic manufacturing products in textiles, garments, electronics, toys, and plastics stimulated rapid economic development (Rabushka, 1979, pp. 16–20; Chenery, Robinson and Syrquin, 1986, pp. 94, 106; Liu, 1992).

More recently, Hong Kong's position as a world-wide trading post has emerged as a key factor in its contemporary economic development as re-exports (rather than domestic exports) became a central focus of economic activity. Indeed, in 1988, the volume of trade in re-exports exceeded domestic exports for the first time in thirty years, and, by 1990, almost 65% of Hong Kong's total exports were re-exports (Ho, 1991, p. 178). Moreover, 58% of the volume of Hong Kong's re-exports originated in China, providing empirical testimony to its growing economic importance to Hong Kong since the economic reforms of 1979 and the 1980s (Sung, 1991a; 1991b).

Yet, data reveals that Hong Kong is going through another economic transformation similar to the changes experienced by other nations that have emerged from manufacturing-based economies: deindustrialization (Ho, 1991, pp. 171–74). In 1980, almost half of Hong Kong's employment was concentrated in the secondary sector (which includes manufacturing and construction). By 1990, the proportion of the work force in the secondary sector had fallen to 36.8% while the proportion of Hong Kong's employment in manufacturing plummeted from 41.7% to only 28% during the same period. The decline in the relative importance of the manufacturing sector is matched by absolute declines in manufacturing workers (Fig. 2.4). Manufacturing employment in the private sector declined from 950,899 in 1981 to only 715,597 in 1990.

In contrast, the tertiary sector (which includes services, finances, trade, etc.) expanded considerably. In 1980, it accounted for only 48.8% of the workforce; by 1990 it claimed 62.1%. The rising importance of the tertiary sector is evidenced by substantial increases in

Figure 2.4: Private Employment by Sector

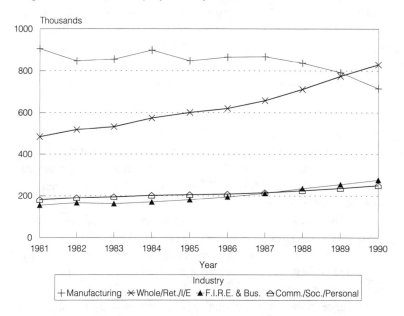

Source: Hong Kong Census and Statistics Department.

jobs in the service sector. Private sector employment in wholesale, retail, import/export trades, restaurants and hotels increased from 483,818 in 1981 to 829,591 in 1990. The number of private employees working in community, social and personal services also rose dramatically, increasing from only 181,205 in 1981 to 250,241 in 1990. During the same time period, private employment in finance, insurance, real estate and business services rose from 154,769 to 276,621.

Hong Kong's deindustrialization is not as dramatic as the data may suggest at first, however. There is growing evidence that a new division of labour is occurring in the Pearl River Delta, as the Special Economic Zones (SEZs) absorb industrial investment (Y. P. Ho, 1992, pp. 234–35; Law, 1992, pp. 152–54). Hong Kong, in fact, is becoming more integrated into the economic structure of China. Moreover, a substantial portion of this investment is in Guangdong. Indeed, Hong Kong industrialists have gained considerably from investment in the Pearl River Delta because wages are 50–70% lower and factory rents are only one-third of Hong Kong levels (Sung, 1991b, p. 101). Moreover, production costs may be substantially lower in outlying rural areas.

Hong Kong investors account for over half of the contracted foreign investment in China (Table 2.1). Hong Kong's share of total foreign investment has consistently remained above 40%, far outpacing the shares of the United States and Japan, the next largest investors (Sung, 1991b, pp. 99–100). Moreover, Hong Kong has been able to weather periods of uncertainty better than others countries, suggesting the Hong Kong investor is "better adapted to China's investment environment than foreign investors" (Sung, 1991b, p. 100).

The emerging role of the tertiary sector should not be underestimated. As Hong Hong becomes a global centre for finance and advanced services, property markets are achieving a unique prominence in the economy relative to other countries. Hong Kong's

Table 2.1: Hong Kong Investment in China

(US$ millions)

Year	Foreign investment		Foreign loans		Total	
	Total amt. (US$)	% from HK	Total amt. (US$)	% from HK	Total amt. (US$)	% from HK
1979–82 Avg.	1,384	66	1,240	7.6%	2,624	38.6
1983	1,917	34	1,513	7.5	3,430	22.0
1984	2,875	76	1,916	15.7	4,791	51.7
1985	6,333	65	3,534	16.6	9,867	47.8
1986	3,330	53	8,401	21.2	11,737	30.3
1987	4,319	54	7,817	35.8	12,136	42.3
1988	6,189	65	9,814	25.7	16,002	41.0
1989	6,294	58	5,184	13.8	11,479	42.3

Source: Sung, 1991b, p. 18, Table 2.2.

property and construction industries represent 45% of the capitalization in the Hong Kong stock market, significantly higher than in Singapore (13%), Malaysia (8%), Japan (under 2%), and the United Kingdom (under 10%) (Walker, *et al.*, 1990, p. 26). Moreover, over 60% of Hong Kong's investment expenditure is in the form of property and about 30% of all bank lending is to the property and construction industries (Walker, *et al.*, 1990, pp. 29–31; 1991, pp. 34–36).

Indeed, the proportion of bank lending to property and residential markets has increased over the past decade (Table 2.2). Data collected by the Census and Statistics Department reveal that 32% of the loans made by Hong Kong's licensed banks went to building construction, property development or private purchases of residential units (either through the Home Ownership Scheme, Private Sector Participation Scheme, or purchases of other residential property) in 1981. The

Table 2.2: Property and Development Loans in Hong Kong Licensed Banks, 1981–91

(HK$ millions)

Year	Building, construction, & property development	Private residential purchases	Total loans	Percent property related loans
1981	24,123	8,927	103,375	32.0
1982	36,192	11,386	137,118	34.7
1983	37,194	14,571	161,873	32.0
1984	39,332	17,001	176,231	32.0
1985	33,813	22,280	192,009	29.2
1986	31,265	32,335	228,202	27.9
1987	36,909	47,555	307,077	27.5
1988	54,899	66,892	406,693	29.9
1989	92,429	89,869	530,019	34.4
1990	103,116	116,674	620,189	35.4
1991*	115,660	148,483	700,271	37.7

* Through September 1991
Source: Hong Kong Census and Statistics Department.

proportion of total loans going to the property development market has increased, after dipping in the mid-1980s, to 35.4% in 1990 and 37.7% at the end of the third quarter in 1991. Thus, while the value of total loans made by licensed banks increased 577% during this period, the value of loans made to the property development industry and residential purchases increased by 699%. Moreover, this growth was fueled in large part by a substantial increase in loans to private individuals to purchase residential property. The amount of such loans rose from $7.983 billion in 1981 to $138.141 billion through September 1991.

The boom in the property market was also reflected in the stock market (Table 2.3). The Hang Seng Index increased 311% from 1984 to 1991, largely as a result of the property market boom. Among the sub-indices, the properties sub-index grew by 545%, out-performing finance, utilities and commerce and industry over this period. Only the utilities index performed better than the total index, increasing by 377%.

As the Hong Kong economy matures, the property market will likely become even more important as the industry attempts to meet the demand for high-quality residential and commercial development. The expanding role and influence of the tertiary sector is a healthy

Table 2.3: Hang Seng Index and Sub-indices, 1984–91

Year	Hang Seng Index	Finance	Utilities	Properties	Commerce & industry
1984	1,008.54	991.86	1,128.80	1,063.54	910.54
1985	1,567.56	1,290.4	1,902.98	1,952.31	1,376.6
1986	1,960.06	1,379.74	2,659.87	2,435.92	1,759.33
1987	2,884.88	1,933.37	6,594.42	4,257.11	2,536.89
1988	2,556.72	1,625.59	3,486.63	3,847.90	2,317.96
1989	2,781.04	1,808.10	3,198.71	4,535.15	2,686.98
1990	3,027.47	1,906.92	3,840.58	4,874.47	2,797.00
1991*	4,149.80	3,043.59	5,384.38	6,867.39	3,406.77

* Through November 1991
Source: Hong Kong Census and Statistics Department.

indicator of the Hong Kong economy's ability to respond to market signals. Rather than lamenting the loss of manufacturing jobs to Shenzhen, Hong Kong entrepreneurs have quickly and easily converted existing resources into more productive uses.

Property Markets, Fiscal Discipline and Economic Growth

The Hong Kong economy does not exist in a policy vacuum, however. Indeed, as the experiences of developing economies in Latin America, Africa, and Asia demonstrate, economic development is not easily achieved. Most developing countries have experimented extensively with non-market mechanisms in order to stimulate their economies. Despite large infusions of capital and extensive economic planning, the majority of these countries found their economies falling even further behind the industrialized countries as a result of these attempts at stimulation, and their efforts rewarded by further stagnation and, in too many cases, political unrest. Ironically, Hong Kong, Singapore, South Korea, and Japan prospered because they pursued economic development strategies contrary to the "best" advice from development experts in the post-World War II era.

In fact, Hong Kong and the other Asian Dragons would never have progressed as rapidly if they had adhered to the advice of conventional development economists in the 1950s and 1960s. Development theory, according to one of its more renowned critics, was caught in a "dirigiste dogma" that rejected free markets and trade as a mechanism for promoting economic development, substituting in their place centralized government planning, regulation, public investment and import-substitution (Lal, 1985). The result was a general decline in living standards and the quality of life (see Bauer, 1984; Lal, 1985; Little, 1982). The Asian Dragons, in contrast, embraced markets, foreign investment, the private sector, and export-oriented growth as the principal mechanisms for their ascendance from poverty.

The apparent superiority of markets in promoting economic development was eventually acknowledged by international organizations such as the World Bank, one of the principal institutions that initially encouraged the move toward price controls, import substitution, and planning in developing countries. Top-down planning in developing countries distorted prices, allowed political decisions to override market decisions, created economy-wide inefficiencies, low productivity, and stagnant growth. "There is no clear association between a high degree of planning efforts and their performance in terms of growth," observes a World Bank analysis of the impact of planning on Third World countries (Agarwala, 1983, p. 2). "The basic political assumption," observes internationally respected development economist I.M.D. Little in his summary of the effects of planning in developing countries, "was that the LDC governments ... were strong, wise, and undivided, and that their sole objective was the welfare of their people. This did not turn out to be true." (1982, p. 58)

How did Hong Kong escape the dirigisme of the mid-twentieth century? To some extent, its economic performance is a function of its geographic location and historical place as a territory in a declining empire. Even more important in explaining Hong Kong's ascendance towards a thriving economy, however, was the role of public policy and the importance of maintaining a booming economy to ensure political stability and effective governance. Hong Kong is firmly committed to an economic system geared toward maximizing output and efficient use of the economy's resources. Most policy proposals have been subjected to evaluations that consider the impact on the "automatic corrective mechanism" of the price system. "Given Hong Kong's unusually high degree of external orientation," notes economist Yin-ping Ho, "all relevant public policy decisions must have regard to the need to safeguard the efficiency of the self-regulation [market] mechanism so as to maintain external competitiveness." (1992, p. 202)

The commitment to free markets and free trade has also enabled the government to avoid interventionist policies that would have undermined future development. Sociologist Lau Siu-kai has observed that Hong Kong's healthy economy has allowed the government to pursue a more benign role in society and economy. It is important to note, Lau emphasizes, that the apparently non-political nature of Chinese culture and society has been interrupted by rare, but important, periods of political activity and instability. In Hong Kong, riots have erupted in 1956, 1966, and 1967. The Tiananmen Square incident in 1989 also resulted in political activism. Expectations of a rising standard of living have helped mute political activism among the Hong Kong Chinese. As long as the populace is content with the behaviour of government and public policy, political conflict is diffused.

> The enormous economic success which Hong Kong has achieved enables the government not only to justify its acclaimed laissez-faire economic doctrine, it also affords it the luxury of not being required to play an active interventionist role in society, a luxury denied to many developing countries.... While political in-stability in many developing countries emanates from the failure of their governments to develop their economies and improve the standard of living of the people, the success of economic development in Hong Kong is on the contrary the cornerstone of its political stability. (Lau, 1984, p. 177)[9]

Moreover, given past experience, there is little reason to suspect that the Hong Kong economy will falter significantly barring ill-advised intervention by China after 1997.

The Hong Kong government's adherence to international trade

---

9. Lau believes that much of Hong Kong's economic development is unique to the situation of the territory: "Hong Kong is unique in the sense that the essential ingredients of economic development, whose nonavailability or shortage has retarded the progress of development in many countries and made the public sector indispensible, converged in Hong Kong in the late 1940s and 1950s ... at a time when they were desparately needed to enable her to feed and employ the rising population." (1984, p. 177) The argument in this analysis, in keeping with several other analyses, is that Hong Kong's economic success was achieved because of a non-interventionist policy approach. Indeed, experience from other countries sug-gests that many resources necessary for economic development, such as entrepreneurial labour, exist in other developing countries, but public policies prevent their productive use. See, for example, the analysis in Bauer (1984, particularly pp. 1–18).

and free markets may be directly linked to its ability to directly and tangibly profit from a robust economy since the "pay-offs" to the government from a healthy economy are immediate. Significantly, many of these benefits derive from the government's control over land and property development. Since all the land on Hong Kong Island, Kowloon and the New Territories is controlled or owned by Britain (until 1997), the Hong Kong government benefits directly from the "sale" of leases to private investors, developers, and prospective owners. In booming economic times, government revenues from land sales can be significant (Table 2.4). Land "premia", the revenues received from leaseholders developing their land more intensely, have become an important source of public revenue and make up a substantial portion of the revenues accumulating in the Capital Works Reserve Fund. Revenues from auctions and other land transactions can account for a substantial portion of government revenues in any given year, varying from less than 1% to 35% in any given year.[10] Yeh (1992, pp. 9–10) recently estimated that 55% of the government's total land-related expenditures were covered by revenues from land sales in the period between 1974 and 1990.

The government also collects revenues from property-related transactions, including general rates, profit taxes, stamp duties, and property taxes (Table 2.5). While detailed data on revenues are difficult to obtain, revenues from property-related sources have increased steadily over the last decade. Given the importance of the property market in Hong Kong's economy, a significant share of profits taxes are considered "property related". Taxes on company profits provide the largest share. Such taxes comprise 45% of the government's

---

10.   In accordance with the Joint Declaration, half of the revenues from land sales are placed in a SAR Land Fund that can be tapped only after 1997. Until China formally assumes control over Hong Kong, the government's ability to auction new leases is circumscribed by the Joint Declaration and Basic Law to reduce incentives for the government to increase land sales or incur public debt for political reasons.

Table 2.4: Selected Sources of Government Revenues, 1980–91

(HK$ Millions)

Fiscal year	Operating revenues	Profits & earnings	Stamp duties	General rates	Property & investment
1981/82	24,014	10,567	2,168	484	315
1982/83	24,882	11,849	1,391	697	348
1983/84	27,251	11,423	1,094	1,156	445
1984/85	30,581	13,515	1,157	122	457
1985/86	36,462	16,603	1,696	1,770	516
1986/87	41,894	18,751	3,045	1,188	625
1987/88	53,555	24,772	5,237	1,373	761
1988/89	64,302	29,662	5,095	1,517	2,152
1989/90	73,430	33,549	5,464	1,663	2,337
1990/91	81,400	36,341	5,939	3,039	1,341

Source: Annual Digest of Statistics, Table 8.2, p. 119

Table 2.5: Government Revenues from Land Transactions, 1981–91

(HK$ millions)

Year	Land transactions	Capital works reserve fund	Total revenues	Percent land sales
1981/82	9,676.5	—	35,846.5	27.0
1982/83	5,048.1	—	32,267.7	15.6
1983/84	2,267.1	—	32,813.2	6.9
1984/85	4,267.2	—	38,511.1	11.1
1985/86	3,894.6	586.4	43,695.3	10.3
1986/87	755.6	2,330.9	48,602.7	6.4
1987/88	461.3	3,513.4	60,876.9	6.5
1988/89	364.6	6,393.0	72,658.5	9.3
1989/90	212.0	7,457.8	82,430.2	9.3
1990/91	241.1	4,002.5	89,523.8	4.7

Source: Hong Kong Census and Statistics Department.

operating revenues in any given year, and tripled from 1981/82 to 1990/91. Revenues from property taxes, general rates and stamp duties make up another 13% of total government revenues. Calculations by Walker and Flanagan (1991, pp. 68–69), suggest that the property market typically contributes 40–50% of stamp duties and between 13 and 17% of profit taxes. Overall, property-related items have contributed almost 40% of all revenues to the government during the 1980s, varying from as much as 60% in 1980 to only 27% in 1986.

From the perspective of the Hong Kong government, then, a healthy, robust property market is essential to maintain its revenues. Interventions that interfere with the economy's ability to adapt to economic changes (or compromise the automatic adjustment mechanism) will have impacts on government revenues. Hong Kong balances its budgets over business cycles, which has resulted in virtually no public debt until the Port and Airport Development Strategy (PADS) was undertaken. In fact, Hong Kong has been able to generate fiscal surpluses as a result of its conservative fiscal policy. These net surpluses "have enabled the government to finance many a large infrastructural project essential to long-term industrial development" (Y. P. Ho, 1992, p. 196). Any disruption in the governments revenues stream could impact public investment in routine infrastructure, including highways, sewers, water systems, the new airport, etc. Given Hong Kong's strict adherence to balanced budgets, tampering with the territory's economy will also have dramatic and significant impacts on the ability of the government to follow through on public projects such as the new airport, light rail transport system, and container terminals.

Town Planning in Hong Kong

The emergence of a significant property market and structural changes in the Hong Kong economy have important implications for land-use planning and regulation in Hong Kong. Industrial investment has been shifting to the Pearl River Delta and its hinterland to take advantage of low-cost labour. Thus land development in Hong Kong has shifted toward development and redevelopment of commercial property, particularly on Hong Kong Island and in Kowloon. Flexibility in property development and price competitiveness are essential for ensuring that Hong Kong can position itself to take advantage of changes occurring in world financial markets. Similarly, a flexible and smoothly functioning property market is essential if Hong Kong expects to maintain economic growth. A cornerstone of past economic development has been the stability of property rights engendered by a commitment to non-interventionism by the Hong Kong government.

This foundation for economic growth, unfortunately, may be compromised if current reforms in town planning are implemented. New rules, regulations, and restrictions on land-use will disrupt the process of land development and adjustment in Hong Kong. To the extent the powers given to town planners allow for more governmental control and direction over development, uncertainty will increase in property markets and destabilize the system of property rights. Future economic growth may be compromised.

The Hong Kong system of town planning is far less complex, bureaucratic, and intrusive than the systems in the United States, United Kingdom, or virtually any other industrialized country. Hong Kong avoids detailed controls over future development, relying on broadly defined zoning classifications and occasional plan making. While systems in countries such as the United States and the United Kingdom have become burdensome, politicized, and cumbersome, the Hong Kong planning system is "growth friendly". Developers can expect to begin and complete their projects in far less time than can their colleagues in other countries.

Development control is exercised primarily through the Planning Department's advisory role in the Buildings and Lands Department and lease conditions. The primary criteria for approving plan applications has been whether the project conforms to building codes geared toward public health and safety concerns and the conditions of the lease. While the Planning Department has had success in imposing more limits on development in recent years, development control is far more constrained in Hong Kong than in other countries. This role, however, appears to be changing significantly.

Non-interventionism and Town Planning

Historically, the government's policy of relying on the "automatic corrective mechanism" of the market and allowing export-driven growth to lead economic development has been referred to as "positive non-interventionism" (see Miners, 1991, pp. 47–49; Rabushka, 1979). In fact, many independent observers credit Hong Kong's "positive non-interventionism" as an important factor in its success (Bauer, 1981, pp. 185–90; Sowell, 1983, p. 232; Sen, 1984, pp. 101–103, 486–88; Sowell 1987, pp. 89–91; Y. P. Ho, 1992, pp. 27–28). Within a broad framework of common law that protects private property rights, Hong Kong remained true to its heritage as a trading post by creating an environment favourable to entrepreneurship and business enterprise. As a rule, the government pursued a "hands off" policy with respect to businesses, avoiding tariffs and trade duties, maintaining a simple tax structure, allowing for the free flow of international capital, and minimizing business regulation. The result was the emergence of a stable system of property rights that protects private property, profits, and investment. Within this context, Hong Kong's emergence as one of the world's pre-eminent business and financial centres is not surprising.

Importantly, this non-interventionist approach to economic policy and international trade paralleled a non-interventionist philosophy in public administration of planning. The government has broad legal powers to regulate land-use in the "public interest". These powers are described generally in the 1939 *Town Planning Ordinance* as well as in literature produced and distributed by the Hong Kong Planning Department. Yet, the government has not aggressively pursued planning objectives through legislation. Rather, it has relied on detailed restrictions of leases (particularly since the 1960s) put up for public auction, statutory land-use plans, and the enforcement of buildings codes through the *Buildings Ordinance* (1955). These restrictions and building codes have been supplemented by more detailed zoning plans and explanatory statements that restrict land-use development. Over the years, the willingness of local planners to abide by the established approach to regulating land-uses (through lease restrictions, building regulations and zoning) has provided a stable and flexible framework for property markets to adapt to the changing needs of Hong Kong and the world economy. Deviations from published plans have been relatively few and, for the most part, have not affected existing or impending development.

Pressures for Political Change

In recent years political events seem to be pushing the people and government of Hong Kong into a more interventionist policy stance. The current Financial Secretary, Hamish Macleod, for example, has explicitly and publicly rejected positive non-interventionism as not being realistic in the modern world economy. "Some have described me as more interventionist in approach," noted Macleod in a recent article in the *South China Morning Post*. "I don't mind this. Indeed, I have never liked the phrase positive non-interventionism, which outlived its usefulness years ago." (1992) Indeed, Macleod speaks for many citizens and public officials when he observes that "Hong Kong has become more sophisticated. The Government is doing more and more, and that is very much a fact of life." (1992) While the government still "believes" in the market system, everything, including property markets, cannot always be trusted to markets.[11]

The rejection of positive non-interventionism and the apparent willingness of the government to become more interventionist in the internal workings of the economy will be reinforced by other political changes. One of the more important political reforms, for example, has been the push to make government more representative and accountable, a result of the impending transfer of sovereignty to China in 1997 and a series of White Papers released by the government from 1984 to 1988. Among the more salient trends has been a

---

11. Hong Kong does not appear to have significantly moved away from a conservative fiscal policy approach despite recent controversies surrounding financing for PADS. Nevertheless, as the following chapters suggest, there is substantive evidence that planners are likely to become increasingly more interventionist.

push for an increase in direct representation through the electoral process (Miners, 1989). The general public will have more direct influence over the legislature.

The Legislative Council (LegCo), in particular, is going through radical changes in its representation (Miners, 1991, pp. 114–17). The first elected representatives appeared in 1985, but all these members represented "functional constituencies" (business, professional and labour organizations). By 1995, all appointed members of the council will be replaced by members elected from either functionally or geographically based constituencies. After 1997 the political structure of the SAR government will be governed by the Basic Law promulgated in 1990, which provides for a process of gradual political evolution. By 2003, LegCo will consist of 60 members, 30 representing functional constituencies, 20 elected directly from geographical constituencies, and 10 returned by an election committee. Since the Tiananmen Square incident, pressures for moving the government toward more direct democracy and representation before 1997 have intensified.

Even if the restoration of sovereignty to China in 1997 has not made political changes inevitable, such changes, as well as an increase in activism, would no doubt have occurred as a result of economic growth and development. Hong Kong's economic growth has been accompanied by problems that are by-products of successful economic development. In essence, as Hong Kong's wealth and income has grown, its politicians and planners have become more sensitive to the "social costs" of growth.[12] Minimizing these social costs, some believe, requires the abandonment of positive non-interventionism, particularly with respect to planning and land-use regulation. Yet, the conventional tools of town planners to control for these factors are fundamentally inconsistent with providing a "growth-friendly" economy. This inconsistency is explained further

---

12. In fact, economic growth and development leads to more political activism in virtually every culture. See the discussion on political activism and economic status in Lau (1984).

in Chapter 4. Before embarking on this discussion, however, a fuller understanding of how local planning has been implemented is necessary.

CHAPTER 3

Local Planning and Economic Development

Town planning is often considered a tool for enhancing the quality of life for people living in built-up urban areas. Real estate markets, when left untended, are capable of marshalling vast amounts of resources into productive activities, providing a foundation for rising living standards and material improvement in the quality of life. Market driven economies, however, also tend to produce seemingly disorderly or haphazard patterns of development that compromise intangible, non-material aspects of human life. Thus, while the market may register the value of a plot of land for a commercial developer, it tends to overlook, if not ignore, the social costs of lost green space, environmental impacts, congestion and other by-products difficult to measure or specify in contracts.

Town planning, through development controls and land-use regulation, provides an alternative to the hectic, externality-ridden pace of market-driven development. Town planners, through their forward looking posture and willingness to clamp down on narrowly focused private interests, can manage future development to ensure that society reaps the maximum benefits from economic development.

In most cases, planners are not attempting to stop growth. Rather, they are attempting to control it by channeling the productive energies of private interests in socially productive directions. Thus, rather than calling a halt to commercial or industrial development, planners attempt to direct such development to the areas for which it is most suitable. Rather than preventing a commercial office building from being constructed, planners are concerned that the design of the building meet's "community standards" or is "consistent" with the development of the neighbourhood. Rather than telling firms who they can hire or what inputs they should use in production, planners and town planning will help ensure the "appropriate" economic development, suitable to the economic and social needs of the community occurs.

Unfortunately, as the following sections explain, the theoretical framework and practical tools of town planners are inconsistent with their goals. Modern town planning is fundamentally inconsistent with market-driven economic development, particularly the type that is inherent in Hong Kong's shift to advanced services. To a great extent, this is a result of a misunderstanding of the role and function of markets in economic development. Indeed, a deeper, more comprehensive understanding of the market might lead modern town planners to view their role in a different light and develop tools that aid rather than hinder economic development.

But, general discussions of town planning tend to obscure important differences in the ways in which planning principles are applied in the real world. While a careful perusal of planning textbooks finds little difference in the theoretical frameworks employed by planners throughout the world, substantial variation exists in the practice of planning in communities and in different countries. These differences reflect, in part, variations in the legal framework, culture, and political importance of professional planners (on national, regional, and local levels).

Yet, variations in planning practice can also provide important insights into the factors that affect planning implementation and its potential impacts on economic development. Thus, this chapter focuses on the practice of town planning in the United States, a decentralized fragmented system encompassing tens of thousands of local governments, and in the United Kingdom, a system that has been defined in large measure by the importance of planning issues as national policy. The experiences of these countries, in addition to planning experience in Hong Kong, will be used to provide the general background for critically assessing the weaknesses of town planning to control economic growth.

Planning Experience in the United States

In the United States, a highly fragmented and decentralized system of planning has evolved (see Popper, 1988). This is, to some extent, a reflection of a federal governmental structure. The Ninth and Tenth Amendments (part of the Bill of Rights) to the United States Constitution restrict the power of the federal government to infringe on the rights of states and citizens. "The powers not delegated to the United States by the Constitution," warns the Tenth Amendment, "are reserved to the States respectively, or to the people." As a result, since planning responsibilities are not enumerated as a power of the federal government, planning and land-use regulation have been exercised primarily by local authorities.[1]

Federal involvement in city and regional planning has tended toward providing "carrots" to encourage communities to establish general plans and adopt zoning. In 1922, federal legislation encouraged the adoption of comprehensive plans through the *Standard State Zoning Enabling Act*, but only communities seeking aid or assistance from the federal government had to meet these requirements. When large scale public works projects were undertaken by the federal government in the 1930s and 1940s, planning became a vital ingredient in efforts to revitalize American cities through New Deal and war-related programmes. Federal incentives became even more important when federal legislation strengthened the government's hand in housing, authorizing federal funds to subsidize urban renewal (redevelopment) in American cities only if the projects were part of a general comprehensive plan. In the 1950s and 1960s, the federal government encouraged local governments to develop plans by funding the plan-making process directly. Throughout the history of local planning in the United States, however, the federal role has been subservient to local initiative and intent.

---

1. This restriction on federal intervention in land-use has been eroding over the years. The primary focus of rising federal interest in land-use regulation and local planning has been through environmental regulations. See Propst (1991).

Legally, United States Courts have granted wide discretion to local authorities in planning decisions. Planning and land-use regulation have been broadly supported as legitimate functions of states and localities, and have remained outside the province of federal authority and intervention. For example, courts have allowed cities to tightly regulate land-uses as long as the regulation did not entirely deprive the landowner of economic use.[2] Increasingly, courts have upheld the authority of local jurisdictions to abrogate the property rights of landowners as long as the regulation can be justified as benefiting the public interest. Over time, the judicial standards for limiting public "takings" through planning and zoning regulations have become more relaxed as cities have used increasingly broad definitions of public interest (Schultz, 1992; Paul, 1987; Epstein, 1985), and the courts have deferred to local public opinion in defining public purpose (Fischel, 1985, pp. 39–58). In one case, the city of Detroit seized 1,176 buildings and displaced 3,500 people by using its powers of eminent domain to provide 465 acres for a new automobile assembly plant. The courts ruled that the interests of the city in promoting economic development outweighed the interests of private residents (see the discussion in Schultz, 1992, pp. 99–107). While recent court cases have strengthened the hands of property owners (Singer, 1992) there is, little evidence to suggest that the federal courts will move to strengthen private property rights much further (Schultz, 1992).

The central government's "hands-off" approach to city planning and zoning has given planners substantial discretion in implementing detailed, comprehensive planning on the local level. Some local planning systems are so extensive that the cities are referred to as "planned communities." Planned communities are common in the southwest, particularly in California, although East Coast cities such as Reston, Virginia and Columbia, Maryland are credited as the first completely planned communities (see Garreau, 1991). Moreover, movements among planners indicate that some regions of the United States are

2. As Chapter 6 discusses, this has important implications for property rights in the context of compensation.

more positively disposed toward local planning, resulting in a concentration of planners in particular areas of the country (Popper, 1988).

On the other hand, some communities in the United States are entirely or almost entirely unplanned. In many rural areas, local residents view zoning and planning as an infringement on their property rights, and resist attempts from neighbouring and regional governments to impose comprehensive planning systems. Some cities, among which Houston may be the most notable, have avoided significant and sophisticated zoning systems altogether (see Seigan, 1972).

Unlike other countries and cities such as the United Kingdom and Hong Kong, the United States is characterized by substantial undeveloped territory, allowing for a wide degree of choice and mobility among residents, businesses, and industry. As a result, many people move to local jurisdictions that conform to their "preferences" for planning and zoning.[3] Some residents choose highly regulated and planned communities because those areas might provide more stability and continuity, while others choose more relaxed rural or semi-rural communities that might be less rigid and doctrinaire about land use. The amount of land and a well maintained interstate highway system provides relatively easy access to communities and facilitates this type of mobility as well.

The case of zoning provides a telling illustration of the diversity of land-use and planning systems within the United States. Many rural areas allow virtually any piece of land to be developed for whatever purpose its owner believes appropriate. A typical zoning map (if one exists) for an unincorporated area will include three designations: residential, industrial, and commercial. Land that is not in one of these districts is almost always agricultural. Usually, the

---

3. The concept that residents "vote with their feet" to search for cities with "preferred" levels of public service was pioneered by Tiebout (1956). A substantial literature has developed in the public finance literature addressing the "Tiebout Effect" and its implications for residential mobility.

number of always permitted uses is wide and land-use regulations are flexible (and even negotiable).

Larger jurisdictions, on the other hand, often have extremely complex zoning laws and extensive development controls. Mid-size cities that have a professional staff (usually a city manager or planning director) will divide land-uses more specifically (see Fig. 3.1). Residential districts may be divided based on their density, or according to whether they consist of multi-family or single family uses. Districts can be categorized further according to their lot sizes, the minimum floor area allowed a single dwelling, minimum curb length, etc. The residential district R-1AA in Figure 3.1 specified that lots must be at least five acres with a minimum floor area of 1,500 square feet per dwelling.

Commercial zones might be similarly subdivided into professional office, service office, retail, wholesale, or food establishments. The city of Dayton, Ohio, for example, with a population of 180,000,

Figure 3.1: Selected U.S. Zoning Classifications

Zoning District	Description of Use
R-1AA	Single family, large lot
R-1A	Single family, mid-size lot
R-1B	Single family, small lot
R-2	Two family residential
R-3	Multi-family residential
B-1	Highway business
B-2	Convenience shopping
B-3	Neighborhood business
B-4	Central business district
O-1	Office buildings
I-1	Industrial uses
A-1	Agricultural uses

has twenty-three zoning districts: nine residential, five commercial, three industrial, and six special districts. Neighbouring Springfield, with a population half the size of Dayton, has twenty districts: eight residential, five commercial, four industrial, one planned unit development, and three special districts.

Large cities have a dizzying array of land-use regulations and zoning codes, typically in excess of 50 land-use categories. Cities as large as Chicago or New York may find their land-use designations growing astronomically. In addition to designating various sub-districts, municipalities may create "special districts" to protect historical landmarks, recreational areas, schools, certain residential areas, flood control areas, etc. Zoning and land-use regulations can govern everything from constructing a new building to the colour the front door may be painted. Many suburban communities, for example, impose fines on residents whose grass grows higher than the legal limit.[4]

Since the late 1960s, many cities and communities have resorted to more direct and complex controls over development.[5] Using zoning and other planning tools, certain communities have limited

---

4. Moreover, land-use plans and zoning regulations are rarely overhauled. New York City's plan has had over 2,500 amendments and has not been overhauled since the mid-1950s (Horsely, 1974) and continues to be one of the most obstructionist and complex systems in the U.S. (see Hochman, 1988). Even smaller cities do not revise their zoning codes often. Fort Collins, Colorado, for example, developed its zoning map in 1929 and this map was not updated until the 1960s. Eventually, the city dropped its conventional zoning system because it was too rigid and cumbersome (Eggers, 1990a). A recent analysis of a mid-size metropolitan area in Ohio found that the most important determinant of the complexity of zoning laws was the date on which the laws were implemented (Dando, 1990). Thus the complexity of the zoning plans increased with their ages.

5. This trend was not universal. Fort Collins, Colorado dropped its conventional zoning and planning system in 1979 in favour of a flexible development system called Land-Use Guidance System. The new system effectively minimizes attempts to centrally plan development in favour of project approvals based on performance zoning. The success of the system has prompted several other communities to develop similar non-zoning systems. See the discussion in Eggers (1990a; 1990b).

economic growth by imposing restrictions on floor area, lot size, set backs, infrastructure requirements, etc. Some communities have even placed moratoriums on issuing building permits. As part of a statewide effort to control urban growth in Florida, cities are required to stop development until the "necessary" infrastructure (e.g., roads, sewer, water) is in place to support the development (Koenig, 1990). The effect has been to bring to a halt new development in some communities, particularly in poorer cities lacking the revenues necessary to finance infrastructure before development takes place. The intent of most growth management programmes, whether statewide or local, is to reduce growth in order to preserve the "quality of life" of the local community.

The effects of increasingly complex development controls have been difficult to measure. Statistical analyses of these controls, however, reveal that the primary beneficiaries are existing residents and homeowners, since property values increase substantially as the housing supply decreases. The authors of a review of the literature on growth controls in the United States conclude that

> In general, growth control measures make owners better off and benefit moderate or high-income families the most. Since the lower income groups are predominantly renters, they experience an increase in housing costs without sharing the capital gains from increased housing prices. (Lillydahl and Singell, 1987, p. 72)

While these inflationary effects may benefit existing homeowners, higher prices place a higher financial burden on new homeowners and renters. In fact, one of the principal consequences of growth controls has been to widen the gap between rich and poor in American metropolitan areas (Downs, 1988). One analysis of 64 communities in the San Francisco Bay area found that the selling price of houses increased by between 17 and 38% in communities with growth control measures (Katz and Rosen, 1987). Another study of 85 cities in North Carolina found that in areas with more complex housing codes families live in less spacious apartments and there was a lower rate of homeownership (Walden, 1990). The result was a decline in the quality of life, particularly for lower income residents.

In fact, growth controls in states such as California on the Pacific Coast and Florida on the Atlantic Coast have caused housing prices to sky-rocket making housing unaffordable to many. A study conducted by the Claremont Institute found that zoning permits, delays, permit conditions, and building codes increased the cost of a typical home in Orange County, California by 80% (Eggers, 1990b, pp. 5–6). Houston, Texas, on the other hand, the only large United States city without comprehensive zoning, has been able to consistently produce more affordable housing than zoned cities such as Dallas, Texas (Seigan, 1990, pp. 27–28; Eggers, 1990b, pp. 5–7). Moreover, Houston has been able to adapt its supply of housing to the changing needs and demands of local residents since developers are unencumbered by local zoning regulations and growth control measures.

Increasingly, the dominant feature of local planning has become political control over property. Indeed, one of the expressed purposes of planning is to override market forces to allow third parties to limit the development potential of some sites. In fact, citizens have increasingly used the ballot box to set land-use policy, particularly in California (Kahn, 1985). In most cases, these referenda are intended to slow or stop economic growth (Longhini, 1985). Zoning laws have also been used to prevent manufacturing sites in central cities from being overtaken by new residential development (King, 1988). In many cases, certain uses may be banned simply because planners do not recognize their economic significance within the community. Zoning laws have been used to squeeze out small, community-based commercial enterprises ("Mom and Pop" stores) as well as specialized businesses such as mini-warehouses. Mini-warehouses allow owners of small professional, service, and retail firms to store inventory more cheaply than by renting space in higher-priced shopping areas. Since mini-warehouses are considered "incompatible" with certain neighbourhoods, they are often banned by local planners, forcing business people and residents to pay higher prices for storage facilities, or to incur higher travel costs. Other potential development sites may be considered historical landmarks and kept from demolition, even if the building in question is unoccupied and in serious disrepair.

Zoning laws have also been used to limit home-based enterprises, significantly compromising the ability of local residents to earn extra income (Pratt, 1987; Williams, 1992a). By zoning districts as residential, mixed uses become illegal neighbourhood dynamics are sometimes destroyed. The power over land development or redevelopment rests, in practice, on the decisions of professional planners. A case study of the Atlanta metropolitan area, for example, found that a very small minority of zoning applications were approved over the objections of local planners. In the vast majority of cases, zoning boards go along with the recommendations of their professional staff (Fleishmann, 1989).

Yet, despite these increasingly complex land-use regulations and growth controls, frustrations over the apparent inability to control development has led several states to impose even more comprehensive planning. State-wide growth controls initiatives have emerged in Oregon, California, Florida and New Jersey, and several other states are considering more comprehensive regional planning to contain urban sprawl, dilute population densities, and reduce competition for development among governments. In Florida, the *Growth Management Act of 1985* requires a moratorium on all new building permits until the local government proves to regional planning authorities that the local infrastructure is capable of supporting the new development (Koenig, 1990). In New Jersey, state-wide planners have selected certain regions as growth centres, or growth corridors (Gusskind, 1988). Local communities are expected to follow state guidelines on how much growth is permitted, when it can take place, and where it is supposed to occur.

Ironically, many of the problems that state-sponsored planning legislation attempts to address may, in fact, be created by the successful application of local planning rules through distortions in property markets and land development. Economist William A. Fischel concludes his extensive survey of the literature on growth controls in the United States by observing

> Inefficiently withdrawing land from development forces builders to look elsewhere in the metropolitan area. The most likely sites are in ex-urban and rural communities, where the political climate,

at least initially, is more favorable to development. As such communities become partly developed, the newcomers take hold of the political machinery, and then they, too, adopt growth controls, sending development still farther from employment and commercial centers. In the long run, employment and commercial centers also disperse from traditional population centers as they find that employees and customers are harder to find. (Fischel, 1989, p. 81)

In fact, most economic growth and job creation is occurring in suburban and ex-urban areas, often referred to as Edge Cities or urban villages (Garreau, 1991). American central cities continue to languish, like their British counterparts, with substantial undeveloped land, while communities in suburban and rural regions grow. Moreover, many of the early suburbs developed in the 1950s have begun to experience population and income declines in the 1990s. Planners and planning theory have provided few insights into ways cities can off-set these declines.

More indicative of the inherent weaknesses of contemporary town planning in the United States is the inability of planning theory and practice to come to grip with the vagaries and uncertainties of the population movements, changes in age structure, and shifts in employment distributions. Many American suburbs exemplify these weaknesses. Though they have some of the most complex and sophisticated systems of local planning in the world, including comprehensive planning, widespread use of zoning and detailed subdivision regulations that guide development toward a predetermined end-state, suburbs find that the visionary end-state of the comprehensive plan developed in 1960 or 1970 is incompatible with real life in 1990 (Hare, 1988; Eggers, 1990b). Most American suburbs, for example, require extensive driving to obtain basic necessities such as health care, food, and clothing. This is a disadvantage for elderly populations. Most also failed to forecast the rise in double-income families, resulting in shortages of day-care facilities. Many communities are finding it necessary to respond to the changing needs of their communities by allowing for "exceptions" to existing zoning rules and master plans. Despite the best efforts of planners in the post-World

War II era to anticipate changes, many suburban communities have failed to provide the necessary physical and community infrastructure to support elderly and dual-income families.

These incongruities simply highlight the inability of town planning to fulfil its goals of ensuring the orderly and efficient development of land in many communities. They are further exacerbated by changes in "conventional wisdom" concerning the precise definition of appropriate uses. Mixed uses, for example, are now acknowledged as socially beneficial and important elements of successful cities, while early planners considered mixed uses an anathema to urban life.

What distinguishes the American system of local planning is its stunning diversity. With over 100,000 municipalities and local governments, cities are continually experimenting with different techniques, thus acting as laboratories for local planning. The federal role in local planning and land-use regulation remains limited; felt mainly in special areas such as environmental regulation or coastal preservation districts. This has proven a blessing, since planning theory and practice were not homogenized by a centralized governmental structure. Indeed, many of the mistakes of traditional planning may have been revealed only much later in a centralized, hierarchical system imposing one model of planning on all jurisdictions.

Planning in the United Kingdom

In contrast to the United States, town planning is much more centralized and hierarchical in the United Kingdom, a reflection of more limited space and the prominence of planning issues in national politics (see McKay and Cox, 1979). Like the United States, however, town planning emerged as an important function of local governments after decades of evolution. Health and safety considerations led to the *Public Health Act of 1875*, which required municipalities to enforce building regulations to protect the public health and welfare. Planning issues were integrated further into building and land-use regulations through the *Housing and Town Planning Act of 1909*.

The most significant expansion of local authority over planning, land use, and economic development issues emerged through the

Town and Country Planning Act (TCPA) *of 1947*. This legislation, riding the cusp of post-war optimism, provided for an integrated system of land-use planning to be implemented on all levels of government (Deakin, 1985; Middleton, 1991). The initial intent was to centrally plan economic development through a top-down, hierarchical system where local planning officials would be responsible for implementing plans developed at the regional and national levels. The TCPA also nationalized virtually all development rights by requiring property owners to apply for development permission before any "material change of use" could be allowed. Any significant development required "express consent" from the local planning authority. Over time, the emphasis on top-down planning faded as the inability of the government to completely control development was revealed and planners moved toward allowing more local citizen participation in local planning decisions in the 1960s and 1970s (Deakin, 1985; Middleton, 1991).

English town planning is now used to guide land development rather than dictate uses. While most strategic planning is performed on the regional and national levels, and must be approved by the Secretary of Environment, the majority of decisions over plan applications and development control are deferred to local planners. This contrasts significantly with other planning systems, such as that of the Netherlands, that are characterized by extremely detailed planning on the local level. In the Netherlands, building controls are directly tied to planning controls, significantly reducing the system's flexibility. In fact, planning applications are judged within the Dutch system almost solely on whether the application conforms to the existing local plan (Thomas, *et al.*, 1983, p. 49). English planners, in contrast, can take into consideration other criteria that may not be in existing plans.[6]

---

6. While this may be an advantage of English planning in some respects, it also may institutionalize uncertainty in the plan application process. Added uncertainty, as Chapter 5 demonstrates, hampers urban development and redevelopment.

The role of British planners is also significantly different from that of their colleagues in the United States. British planning is a product of the "garden city" movement, a utopian vision of a balanced community (Fainstein, 1991). As a result, British planning has tended to focus on ensuring that land-uses are appropriately balanced to conform to a community's vision, and development has focused largely on undeveloped "Green Belt" areas. Given the centralized stature of town planning and the political and administrative support of the national government, British planners have been in a much stronger position to implement their visions of urban development and community compared to planners in the United States.

Unfortunately, the results of over forty years of extensive town planning have been disappointing. The British planning system is vague, cumbersome, and prone to delay. Many of the delays are attributable to the localized nature of the system. While town planning legislation has localized the procedures for approving development plans, little guidance is given to communities concerning the types or purposes of developments that can be approved (Healy, 1992). The result is a substantial degree of discretion regarding planning applications on the local level that make developers vulnerable to the whims of local planners. This, in turn, creates substantial uncertainty in the land development process, discouraging investment and development (Rider, 1980).

Developers often apply for several different types of planning permission, making the development process part of an extended negotiation between developers and local planners. As a result, developers may submit multiple planning applications to local planning authorities, hoping that at least one will be approved (Thomas, *et al.*, 1983, pp. 49–53). For example, a developer may submit two development applications at the same time, hoping one will be approved by the planning authorities. If one application is denied (or considered refused because the local authority did not act on it), the developer will appeal the application, hoping a higher authority will overturn the local decision. In the meantime, the developer will continue to negotiate with local authorities over the plan application still under review. Of course, if the negotiations are successful, the appeal for the first application will be withdrawn. On the other hand, if the applications are denied, the developer will continue to submit plan applications until one is accepted.

An applicant can submit a request to the local planning authority to (1) determine whether the proposed development requires planning permission (whether it would not be a significant change of use); (2) request "outline planning permission" to determine whether the type of development is approved in principle; or (3) submit a detailed planning application that outlines the specific nature and type of the intended development. Development may end up using all three types of permissions rather than run the risk of submitting a detailed application with a high likelihood of being rejected. Given their complex nature, major developments almost always require planning permission. Thus, developers typically forego the first type of plan application since the project will almost always entail a significant change in use. In this case, developers will apply for either outline or detailed planning permission.

Public participation is not required, although planners typically consult other departments, interested parties, and politicians. Some cities may, at their discretion, require public consultation before planning permission is given. While statutory limits exist on local planning authorities with respect to the approval of plan applications, the process of negotiating the details of the project can take years. Thus, the plan application process reflects a lengthy negotiation process rather than a technical evaluation of the application (Evans, 1992).

Once the planning application is received from the developer, registered and published, local planning authorities have several options. The application can be approved, rejected, or accepted with conditions. The option of accepting an application with conditions provides substantial flexibility for English planners, allowing them to negotiate with developers for concessions, many of which can be very specific and restrictive. A development in Oxford, England, for example, was approved with stipulations over the placement of trees and shrubs, use of private garages, and availability of green space for a local playground. Moreover, planning permission is given for a specific period of time, usually five years, after which the developer must resubmit an application if development has not already started. This local discretion has become an important source of uncertainty in the development process and has led to calls for comprehensive planning as a mechanism for improving predictability in local planning (Rider, 1980).

Despite the advantage of having an integrated system of town planning that involves all levels of government, many recent critics have argued that the British planning system has been unable to achieve many of its goals. Indeed, with the emergence of the conservative Thatcher government in 1979, planners and town planning have become much less important in national policy than they were in previous administrations (Glasson, 1992; Healy, 1992). While conservatives have expressed important interests in redeveloping the inner-cities, policy has been geared toward economic development strategies rather than planning control (Chisholm and Kivell, 1987; Fainstein, 1991; Middleton, 1991).

Planning restrictions in the United Kingdom tend to be highly constraining economically, limiting the ability of landowners to redevelop land in response to market signals (Evans, 1992). Town planning policies have thus restricted the ability of developers to respond to the changing needs of residential, commercial, and industrial consumers. Such restriction has contributed to rapidly rising prices and speculative investment in England (Evans, 1992; Martin, 1977). In effect, by reducing the number and variety of land-uses, town planning, like its counterpart in the United States, has encouraged inflation in property markets, particularly in southern England.

Summary of Planning Practice in the United States and United Kingdom

Both the United States and United Kingdom provide valuable insights into the effects of implementing sophisticated zoning and planning on the local level. While the institutional setting of their respective planning systems differs radically, their experiences provide a context for understanding the pitfalls of town planning for economic growth and development.

Both the United Kingdom and the United States systems find that delays and uncertainty are endemic in their systems of development control. United States developers seem to have an advantage over their compatriots in the United Kingdom because of the nation's geographic size and the fragmented nature of the planning system. Unlike their the United Kingdom counterparts, United States developers can "vote" with their investment dollars by locating in communities considered more "development friendly". Indeed, the diversity of local planning culture and community tolerance for new growth may be a crucial factor in sustaining economic development in many metropolitan areas.

This apparent diversity in approach and style is less prevalent in the United Kingdom, where the political system tends to be more hierarchical and centralized. Britain's romance with planning extended into virtually every realm of public and private life in the post-World War II era, and perhaps nowhere was this more evident than in the system of town planning. As a result, town planning is a well established obstacle to economic development in many urban areas, demonstrating a clear willingness and desire to micromanage land development. While town planning authority appears to have become more decentralized (bottom-up driven) in recent decades, local planners are in a powerful negotiating position *vis-à-vis* local developers, and demonstrate a clear willingness to use their power to achieve their goals.

The result, however, in both countries, has been extensive disruption of land and property markets. Particularly in the United Kingdom, land markets have effectively been suspended as town planners, rather than market prices, coordinate development decisions on the local level. This disruption, by increasing uncertainty in the development process and adding costs through delays, negotiation, and stricter adherence to local plans, has increased prices for existing development. The planning systems have reduced the supply of new residential, commercial and industrial space in the areas that experience the highest demand for new development. In practice, growth controls have become mechanisms for ending or significantly slowing growth.

Trends and Prospects

The experiences of the United States and United Kingdom have pushed planners to reconsider their approaches to land-use regulation and economic development. In both countries, for example, planners are searching for more flexible approaches that guide market forces rather than direct market forces. In England, Mordey (1986) notes that town planning has been continually searching for more flexibility and comprehensiveness. Healy (1992) observes that the United Kingdom planning system is beginning to focus on planning as strategic management of land rather than dictating its composition and intensity. This drive for more flexibility is accompanied by a renewed emphasis on citizen participation in planning to minimize the overriding influence of national politicians, administrators, and professional interest groups (Healy, 1992; Deakin, 1985).

In the United States, Hall (1989) has traced dominant themes through American planning history, noting how planning efforts moved from European style attempts to create utopian urban forms, to practical concerns over making cities functional for business interests, back to utopianism in the 1920s and 1930s, and then toward urban renewal and redevelopment in the late twentieth century. Planning theory and practice have always been frustrated by vigorous debates over method, content, and design. While these are usually considered signs of a healthy intellectual pursuit of knowledge and understanding, the debates also highlight the problems of accurately predicting the pattern of urban development or even knowing what attributes of a community are considered desirable. Thus, local planners are unable to develop a common paradigm that unifies the profession toward a common goal. Moreover, experience in the United States suggests that local planners have been largely unsuccessful in their efforts to more efficiently allocate resources.

In response, critics of local planning in the United States have pushed for more flexible forms of land use control such as performance zoning systems.[7] These systems attempt to manage development to ensure certain quality of life criteria are met rather than centrally coordinating land-uses types and functions. City planners in Fort Collins, Colorado, for example, effectively dropped their zoning system in favour of the more flexible, market friendly Land Use Guidance System (LDGS). In place of the zoning system, local planners have implemented a system that evaluates potential projects based on a set of 65 "performance criteria" that focus on design and land-use "buffering" to minimize externalities. To be approved, new developments must meet 65% of the performance criteria. Any developer can propose any type of development as long as it meets the criteria detailed in its land use category defined in the LDGS. The adoption of the new system has significantly reduced delays in plan application approvals while increasing the level of citizen participation in the process (Eggers, 1990a; 1990b). While the LDGS system is still used in only a few dozen communities in the United States, it represents a growing trend toward more flexibility in local planning to accommodate rather than hinder market forces.

The move toward flexibility and market-oriented planning systems is not universal. Many planners are pushing for more active roles in directing urban growth to ensure land development conforms to some optimal pattern. Several planners have criticized local communities for allowing frequent rezonings and zoning variances that amount to spot zoning, corrupting its importance to the planning process. While calling for increased flexibility, many planners also reiterate the importance of ensuring that a sound plan exists and is enforced. English planner Mordey argues:

> Currently local plans are being criticised as becoming too similar to the town maps. Is this so deplorable? At the local level we must surely be site specific.... Ultimately local plans must be a framework for development and control. In which case a

---

7. For a review and analysis of these criticisms, see Nelson (1989) and Eggers (1990b).

thoroughly worked out informative land-use plan is essential. I still maintain that the Town Maps could have been adapted to meet the requirements of today. Perhaps we should go further in this direction and examine the possibility of zoning plans as produced by some of our EEC colleagues. (1986, p. 14)

Indeed, despite the national government's conservative political orientation, many United Kingdom planners detect a renewed emphasis on planning in the national government, which presents opportunities for planners and planning to more actively intervene in the development process (Glasson, 1992). The option of increased planning intervention is also emerging in the United States as planners see a chance to expand their roles in a metropolitan-wide context and address issues such as unbalanced development, inequality, environmental degradation, and metropolitan integration (Blakely and Ames, 1992).

But more active local planning is unlikely to achieve the results contemporary planners expect. If town planners continue to rely on traditional tools for controlling growth — more detailed zoning regulations, more discretion over determining the appropriateness of development, growth controls, etc. — the results will probably mirror past experiences. Moreover, to the extent Hong Kong planners rely on conventional planning tools, the likelihood of achieving success will also be bleak. While the institutional contexts in which town planning is implemented diverge widely between the United States, the United Kingdom, and Hong Kong, the likely results will still be significant disruptions of property markets, reduced economic growth and substantial resource dislocations.

The past failures of local planning, however, were not simply a result of insufficient resources to implement regional and local plans. On the contrary, the economically disruptive impacts of local planning come directly from attempts to impose on the development process a vision inconsistent with consumer preferences tracked and processed through economic markets and the price system. To fully comprehend the failure of local planning to adequately manage or direct resources such that they promote economic development effectively and efficiently requires a more complete understanding of the connection between markets and local planning. This is the subject of the next chapter.

CHAPTER 4

Economic Development and Land Use

Despite the prominence of town planning in the urban development process, surprisingly few scholars or planners have looked at the economic relationship between land, economic development, and town planning. Land markets, for the most part, are viewed by planners as things to control, and planning theorists rarely venture into an analysis of the role and function of market prices in coordinating economic development. Further, the experiences of urbanized Western nations suggests that land-use planning has fallen short of its intended goals. In fact, planning theorists and town planners seem to have few ideas that can rejuvenate urban areas suffering from economic decline. Most recommendations revolve around architecture, design, physical infrastructure, and traditional pump-priming.

Thus, modern planning theory and practice provides little insight into urban economic development. While planners can point to individual projects that may have improved a commercial center or depressed neighbourhood, few cities have seen their economies rejuvenated by these attempts. In a large part, this is because planners misconceive the nature of economic development. In fact, the tools, techniques, and conceptual framework used by planners are fundamentally inconsistent with the requirements for economic growth and development.

Current methods of planning require town planners to forecast future development, determine the content and character of the quality of life, constrain property developers, limit the supply of land, and effectively override economic markets to ensure the planners' vision of a more productive use of resources and socially beneficial pattern of development. Achieving this task requires knowledge and intuition that are not available to planners (or anyone else). Moreover, to accurately forecast and guide urban development to some optimal end-state implies that patterns of economic development are readily observable and the process is deterministic. These characteristics would enable planners to guide and manipulate development to achieve their vision of the end-state.

Unfortunately for town planners, economic growth and development is fluid and changing, continually adjusting to new information revealed by consumers and producers in the market. Sustained economic development requires access to information about supply and demand, flexibility, adaptability, and secure property rights. As the growth of Western industrial countries has demonstrated, only private markets that exist within a stable political, cultural and economic institutional setting that protects private property rights (over government interests) are likely to provide the foundation for sustained economic growth (Rosenberg and Birdzell, 1986). The conventional tools used by modern planners are inconsistent with the efficient functioning of market economies, resulting in an unproductive use of resources, higher prices, and, ultimately, slower growth. Importantly, without an efficient and productive local economy, the "higher values" to which planners aspire are unachievable.

The inconsistencies between the tools of town planners and the nature of urban development can be explained most effectively by developing a more realistic understanding of the nature and function of markets and the price system. The failure of town planning rests not so much in the ends as in the methods and techniques used to achieve them. The next two sections of this chapter delve more deeply into the workings of economic markets, particularly property markets, to explore more thoroughly the inconsistencies of modern planning with respect to economic markets and the relationship between town planning and urban economic development.

The Nature of Land in Urban Development

Planners, for the most part, view land as a fixed resource that can be exploited and spoiled relatively easily. Since the supply of land is fixed, society must be careful that land uses conform to the needs and desires of the community. Without land use controls and other forms of growth management, the likelihood that land will be used inefficiently or unproductively is high since real estate markets are driven by the interests of the speculator who focuses on short-term gain and cares little about the long-term consequences for the community or broader society. In Hong Kong, complaints are levelled against developers who rush to build huge commercial office complexes in former residential areas, selling them off to investors who care little about the added congestion, noise, and strain on local services.

Real estate markets, however, are much more complex than usually depicted in standard planning theory texts. At heart is the issue of value and the nature of land as an economic resource. The economist's perspective provides important insights into the nature of land development that are neglected, or at least underappreciated, by conventional planning theory. Yet, these insights are essential for understanding the process of urban economic development.

An economic approach to property development directly challenges many traditional beliefs about the nature of land development. While the physical supply of land is clearly fixed, economists emphasize that potential uses for land are numerous and diverse (Ingram, 1980). The supply of land "to a particular activity," notes one urban economist, can vary significantly and "will be used for that purpose which yields the higher rent" (Neutze, 1987, p. 379). Rent, in this context, refers to the economic return anticipated by the owner of the land.

Particular lots may be suitable for any number of potential uses, all of which yield different rates of return. For example, suppose someone owns the lease to a parcel of land in old Kowloon. The property currently consists of residential flats built in the 1950s during a period of substantial in-migration from China. Given the extraordinary demand for housing at the time, the flats were built to meet immediate needs and have deteriorated over the years. Thus, the site has become a prime candidate for redevelopment.

In an unregulated property market, the landowner has the option to develop land in several ways: he may use it for a commercial office building, for high density middle-income flats, for low-density luxury flats, as a site for light industry or manufacturing, etc. The landowner will choose the project that yields the highest expected return. If, for example, a Kowloon land developer expects demand for residential flats to continue and, with the relocation of the airport to Chek Lap Kok, height restrictions to be lifted, residential development may be very profitable. On the other hand, expectations concerning higher prices for Class A office space on Hong Kong Island or in Kowloon might suggest commercial development would be more appropriate. The land-owner, of course, also has the option of not developing the land at all if he or she believes the potential returns from delaying redevelopment are significant, an option exercised extensively in many central cities in North America and Europe. Similarly, if the land owner sells his property to a developer, the market price will be determined by expectations about development potential. Debates over land-use and the role of private markets in land development often revolve around the appropriateness of certain developments. If a commercial office building is being developed, for example, planners may push to restrict development to residential uses, arguing that a pressing social need exists for "adequate" and "affordable" residential flats. The market, many will argue, is "ignoring" the needs of potential apartment dwellers in favour of the "quick profits" of commercial development. Implicitly, the argument charges that private developers have overlooked the needs of local residents.

Yet, since every site is faced with a variety of potential uses, property owners calculate expected returns on all alternative projects. Canadian economist David Nowlan emphasizes that the nature of land prices is "really quite simple. It is potential use that determines the highest value, which then becomes market price. The market price, in turn, precludes uses other than the one which creates the highest value." (1977, p. 14) In the case of the hypothetical property in Kowloon, the highest return may be from commercial development.

This does not imply that sites suitable for residential development do not exist. Nor does the decision by the property owner imply that a residential project would not be profitable. The final use reflects a decision that, given existing information about the existing market and expectations about future market conditions, *the most profitable use of this land is to designate it for commercial development.*

The choice among alternative types of development by property owners incorporates "opportunity costs" into the market for land.[1] In fact, the selling price of land is determined by the opportunity costs of development. Whether land will be developed, redeveloped, or undeveloped is determined by expected yields given market conditions, the opportunity costs of development, the value land-owners place on the existing use of the land, and the levels of uncertainty in the development process (Nowlan, 1977; Evans, 1983; Neutze, 1987). The rejection of residential development does not imply disregard for the interests of potential residents. Rather, development reflects market calculations of the most productive use.

Planning Decisions and Market Prices

It is important to note that if market prices do not reflect the true opportunity costs of development (e.g., planners restrict the options available to developers), then distortions occur in real estate markets, severing the relationship between costs and returns. In markets where real estate prices may be significantly distorted, developers may be reluctant to invest, since they are unsure of the potential rate of return from their project. Thus, planning rules can act as significant costs in the development process.

Variations in land prices within regions have been cited as significant determinants of land development. In England, for example, Chisholm and Kivell argue that the "primary problem to be solved with respect to vacant land [in inner-cities] is its price relative to alternative sites" (1987, p. 67). Despite the fact that the Royal Town

---

1. Opportunity costs reflect the economic "costs" of foregoing alternative uses, the value of projects not chosen. The opportunity cost of developing the commercial office building in Kowloon, for example, was the next highest valued use (for example, residential or industrial building).

Planning Institute has concluded that "virtually all land" has the potential to be redeveloped, property developers often opt for green-field sites since vacant land development entails less complexity and less regulation. Similar behaviour has been observed in the United States, where companies and developers have consistently shifted investment beyond built up areas (central city or suburban) to take advantage of lower costs (regulatory and fiscal) for new development.

Clearly, central to the functioning of land markets is price (see Nowlan, 1977). Yet, several planners and scholars have argued that land markets do not exist, basing their conclusions on the belief that, since land is physically fixed, prices cannot effectively allocate resources. What many planners (and interest groups) actually imply is that private markets do not value their specific concerns highly enough, justifying the use of political (rather than economic) mechanisms to allocate land-uses in cities. The question of how efficiently property markets allocate land uses, however, hinges on an understanding of how markets function.

Property Development as a Market Process

Planners and planning theorists often depict real estate markets as short-term, speculative markets, driven by the narrow interests of the land developer. In fact, property development is fundamentally future directed. While existing allocations may seem disorderly or incongruent at any given moment in time, they may in fact reflect orderly development within the context of a dynamic, intertemporal market for development. Thus, some land may not be developed at a current date since it may be more suitable for future development (see Nowlan, 1977, pp. 16–20; Neutze, 1987, pp. 186–87).

For example, several observers of urban development in Hong Kong have noted "pencil stick" building development. This occurs when modern high-rise buildings are constructed in older built-up sections of the territory with lower densities. At first glance, these buildings seem incompatible with the architecture of the local community. Nevertheless, the offices and flats are quickly let. Over time, the profitability of the first stick building leads other investors to redevelop nearby property, erecting modern high-rise residential and commercial buildings. Slowly, through redevelopment, the neighbourhood takes on the characteristics of a high rise, mixed use community. This illustrates the way in which at any given point in time the pattern of urban development might seem chaotic or disorderly when, in fact, it merely reflects the process of urban redevelopment, and an eventual upgrade in the quality of housing and office space, as well as an addition to the total supply of residential and commercial space, which helps to control rent/lease inflation.

The Coordinating Function of Prices

At the heart of the economic conception of real estate markets and urban economic development is the price system. Rather than acting merely as a source of revenues for developers, market prices provide essential information about the relative costs and benefits of developing land for one use compared to another: Market prices coordinate resource allocations in land markets. The price of land informs developers of the relative cost of developing one particular parcel of land as compared to others. The cost of the initial purchase becomes an input cost in the production of a completely new product that will be sold on the market.

For example, if Henderson Land Development Corporation buys a lease to virgin land in the New Territories at auction for HK$500 million, it will attempt to transform this lot into something valued on the market (e.g., a middle-income housing estate). The purchase price of the land will be amortized into the price of the flats when they are sold on the open market. The price will also include construction costs and a profit margin.

On the other hand, the price of land reflects the willingness of consumers to purchase the property once it is developed. While a planner may consider an auto repair shop in a residential building a "nuisance" or "inappropriate use", that repair shop may in fact provide valuable services to residents of the building and the neighbourhood. The repair shop exists because it is able to generate the revenues necessary to pay the lease for that property. In addition, the existence of the auto repair shop, to the extent it generates negative externalities, may also contribute to lower housing prices within the building, allowing rents to remain affordable for existing tenants.

Market prices are determined by both supply and demand, although the supply side of the market usually receives the most attention. Thus, the market price provides a benchmark for land developers to compare the potential costs of development to potential returns when the product is placed on the market.

The profit margin represents the developer's willingness to invest given the tangible costs of development and the risks and uncertainties associated with the development process. As such, the profit margin represents the opportunity costs associated with developing a particular lot and, from an economic perspective, is a legitimate cost of doing business. The profit margin is a crucial element in real estate development and an essential component of the coordinating function of the market.

This view of the role of profits contrasts sharply with most planners' perspective. Oftentimes, planners do not consider the uncertainties and vagaries of real estate development to be legitimate costs of developing land. From a strict accounting perspective, the legitimate costs of developing land include only resources expended in the acquisition and development of the lot for sale on the market.

> However, factors such as the uncertainty of planning permissions, differing perceptions of potential use, imperfect knowledge, negotiating ability and rapid increases in land prices may result in land being acquired well below its full development value. This can result in developers making large profits from the increase in land values which are often wrongly confused with the normal profit necessary to induce developers and builders to undertake development. (Thomas, *et al.*, 1983, p. 64)

But the vagaries of the development process, which include uncertainties associated with the planning procedures, are part of the es-timated costs of development. As such, they are *legitimate costs to the developer* and reflect the opportunity costs of developing one parcel of land versus another. They will also be factored into expectations about potential returns from the development. They can, in this context, be considered normal profits. To exclude elements of the land development process such as planning procedures, increases in prices, existence of imperfect information, etc. is to presume, unrealistically, that land markets perform according to a stylized, static real estate market common in textbooks but virtually absent in real life.

The absence of the purely competitive real estate market does not invalidate the importance of prices and markets in the urban development system. On the contrary, it merely requires the adoption of a more realistic understanding of how markets work and how prices coordinate resources. Disruptions in the property market influence expectations about future revenue streams and the opportunity costs of developing land at a particular moment in time. The market price of land will vary accordingly. An increase in uncertainty over the development potential of land may widen the number of potential uses in the future, encouraging developers to delay development (Titman, 1985), reducing the supply of new units, and, in the long run, causing prices to rise. Thus, to the extent the proposed changes to the *Town Planning Ordinance* increase uncertainty, the effect may be to exacerbate and extend real estate development cycles.

The differences between the economist's and planner's perspective on the role of prices, and their respective approaches to land-use development, reflect different "world views", and different perspectives of the market process. In both causes, their general interpretations of the role and function of property markets are important for assessing their expectations about how reforms in land-use planning and development control will impact economic development and markets for land. From the perspective of the planner, more control over land-use development will allow for a more efficient allocation of resources since the planner will be more able to determine the appropriate pattern and pace of development. The economic perspective — the world view adopted by business owners and property developers — tends to view the planner's interventions as inefficient since they increase uncertainty in the development process and interfere with market signals concerning the optimal use of land implicit in market prices.

The differences between the two perspectives can be seen by analyzing the impact of different patterns in land-use. Figure 4.1 depicts land-use under two different regimes: market-driven development and planning-driven development. Market driven development is characterized by numerous mixed-uses and is constantly in-flux. Districts that are currently residential, may become mixed with the addition of commercial uses, and then evolve into completely commercial uses. In the market-driven environment, buildings may be subdivided by market demand according to consumer preferences. Indeed, in some buildings floors or wings may be devoted to different uses.

Figure 4.1: Market versus Planning Driven Development

MARKET DRIVEN DEVELOPMENT

PLANNING DRIVEN DEVELOPMENT

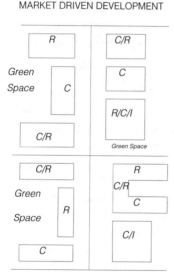
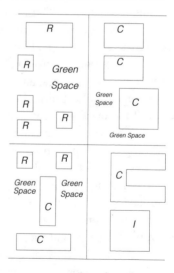

R = residential uses
C = commercial uses
I = industrial uses

Planners would consider this pattern chaotic and disorderly rather than one resulting from real estate markets continually adjusting to the demands and needs of the residents and tenants. In response to this "natural state", planners often impose a static order on development that separates uses and effectively suspends the coordinating function of market prices. Economically compatible land-uses or market-determined densities are not necessarily compatible with planning visions of a well-functioning, orderly urban environment. Thus, uses are separated into districts and, in many cases, densities are reduced to preserve amenities such as open space, or to minimize congestion. Unfortunately, there is no indication that the uses are separated according to the preferences of consumers operating in the market. (Indeed, these preferences are reflected in the "chaotic" pattern of uses in the market-driven scenario.)

Planners, in practice, have often approached the market as something that should be controlled or heavily regulated, presuming the interests of the parties involved in market transactions are independent of long-run considerations or the impacts of others not directly involved in the trade. If land development can be brought under the direct control of a team of trained planners who know and understand society's true and best interests, long-run goals can be set and narrow private interests can be channelled into socially productive investments. Scottish philosopher Adam Smith described the price system as a mechanism for efficiently channelling resources into areas that would best serve consumer needs. In his *Wealth of Nations*, Smith uses the metaphor of the "invisible hand" to describe the process in which the price system, through profits and losses earned in market transactions, requires private investors to produce products and services that meet social needs. Planners have systematically attempted to make the invisible hand visible by explicitly plotting out future development in comprehensive plans for land development.

The Limits to Planning

Unfortunately, comprehensive and master planning is fundamentally incapable of processing efficiently and effectively the millions of diverse bits of information inherent in a freely functioning price system. When developers bid on lots for new development or redevelopment, they make their decisions based on expected costs and revenues. Their success depends on their ability to anticipate consumer wants effectively and to use resources efficiently. If they fail, they lose money and go out of business. If they succeed, they earn profits.

Their decisions are disciplined by the market through the profit and loss system. More importantly, economic decisions are made according to *expected* costs and benefits. Entrepreneurs assess the likelihood of others to participate in the transaction if they invest in the product or service. Typically, small companies can exist to serve small niches of particular markets. This is illustrated by the computer software industry, in which very small firms may dominate certain markets for software applications.

It must be pointed out that, all the relevant information about products, services, costs, and preferences may not exist. The market is driven as much by failure as by success. But, every time a business fails, more information is released to other suppliers and entrepreneurs about the nature of the market. If a land developer builds private flats of 400 square feet or less on Hong Kong Island, he may find that few of his apartments will be rented because customers prefer larger flats. The developer may have to redevelop the site to accommodate larger flats. This failed real estate venture provides important information about what types of residential housing con-sumers want on Hong Kong Island. This information can be used by the existing developer (if he is lucky enough to survive financially) as well as by others developing housing estates on the island and else-where in the territory. The market, in this context, is a discovery procedure (see Hayek, 1978). Through the millions of investments and purchasing decisions that take place in the market, producers and consumers discover new information about the relative costs and the preferences of consumers.

Economic markets are far more inclusive than most planners acknowledge when viewed from the perspective of a dynamic, market process perspective. In fact, market decisions based on the price system are more democratic than their planning counterparts because of the decentralized nature of economic transactions. While developers need to have reasonable expectations about what types of residential, commercial or industrial space is demanded, they do not need to know who the individual consumers will be.

Town planners are fundamentally incapable of processing the types of information that are routinely used in economic markets. Long-term planning, in particular, requires information that does not exist and will not be revealed except through the actual development of land, movement of people, and changes in the structure of the economy. Modern planning presumes that the values of a community are knowable and can be translated into land-use plans that require little modification. In the process, planning eliminates the discovery that is such an important part of economic transactions.

Modern town planning incorporates few procedures for discovering the preferences and values of local residents. As most practitioners can attest, general values about certain processes and trends can be measured using instruments such as community attitude surveys. Surveys can reveal impressions about whether growth is "desirable" in a general sense, or that certain industries are preferred to others. Determining community attitudes on more specific issues is far more difficult and, in many cases, impossible. Planners usually take on the task of interpreting what is socially beneficial and what uses will be allowed or considered appropriate because, in large part, effective mechanisms for revealing preferences are cost-prohibitive or infeasible.

Markets, on the other hand, are extremely efficient at transforming millions of preferences into digestible bits of information through the price system. Developers form expectations about the potential of particular sites based on the successes and failures of projects that preceded them. Since planners do not have effective evaluative procedures, often their decisions come into conflict with market-based decisions.

Take, for example, the case of a private commercial development in Oxford, England (Thomas, *et al.*, 1983, pp. 197–204). The Oxford City Council had a long-standing policy to restrict economic growth, particularly commercial and industrial development. In the early 1970s, a building consisting of 900 square meters that contained printing facilities moved to an industrial estate on the other side of the city. According to the city's development plan approved in 1955, the building lay in an area designated for shopping, general business and parking. It is interesting to note that the owners of the printing business refrained from objecting to this designation during a 1967 review of the development plan because they hoped to receive assistance from the local planning agency and city council when they relocated to a new facility.

> Once the decision had been made to move and approval for the development gained, the old site of Newspaper House became available for development. Clearly, the planning authority saw shopping as the most desirable use for the site. Behind this view, however, lay an anxiety about the difficulties of extinguishing the existing use rights of the site, which would allow new industrial and commercial users to occupy the premises. This would be contrary to the Council's policy of restraining the growth of employment in Oxford. (Thomas, *et al.*, 1983, p. 199)

Since the council had a long standing policy of restricting growth, the city and planning officials were able to place conditions on future development in the area. Aided by zoning restrictions that linked the development plan to the process of development control, local officials had several useful tools for restricting growth. In addition, city council required that only local firms could occupy new office space in the city. Even the selection of the firm that would occupy new space became part of the negotiation for planning permission in Oxford.

In essence, the city suspended the operation of the market. In fact, when a recession led one of the principal tenants in the proposed development to withdraw from the project, the city council refused to allow the private developer to let out space to other potential clients, arguing that demand did not exist outside Oxford to justify changing the permitted use. "So, it was argued, a change in the condition would neither benefit the developer nor Oxford, thus an agreed policy should not be overturned for such scant return." (Thomas, *et al.*, 1983, p. 202)

Similar attempts to override urban land markets occur in other countries such as the United States. Many communities, particularly cities in California, established community redevelopment agencies (CRAs) to revitalize and rebuild "blighted" areas of their cities. As non-profit development agencies, these quasi-government organizations are able to raise funds to demolish entire neighbourhoods and finance new development. They also typically have powers of eminent domain that allow the agencies to condemn private property and seize it for "public purposes". Recently, CRAs have come under fire for abuses of their power to condemn private property, their insensitivity to the desires of local residents, and their willingness to expunge small businesses (Fulton, 1988). Project Area Committees have been created to fight the efforts of CRA's.

Although referenda and litigation have been used extensively is certain parts of the United States to challenge planning decisions, these tools of citizen participation have been weakened in recent years. In Hawaii, for example, the state Supreme Court ruled that a statewide land-use plan overrode the right of residents to challenge planning decisions.

The Shortcomings of Town Planning

Planners are becoming increasingly aware of the shortcomings of their techniques and methods. In a recent edition of *The Practice of Local Government Planning* published by the International City Management Association, general development plans are described as more flexible now than in the past, focusing more on policy issues. "Aspects of fixed land use planning are now used to illustrate the application of policies rather than as a firm statement of the community's future image," the authors observe (Hollander, *et al.*, 1988, p. 71). Increasingly, planners realize that planning as a mechanism to achieve an end state is unrealistic. In fact, general plans are not implemented comprehensively. Rather, they "are implemented through a series of incremental decisions rather than through major construction programmes that rely on the plan as a static blueprint for the future" (Hollander, *et al.*, 1988, p. 71). Indeed, in the modern application of planning, particularly in the United States, the purpose of the general plan is to focus on the *process* rather than the result.

These trends are also detectable in Europe. In England, a decline in the confidence of planners to "plan the future direction of social change in a comprehensive and centralized fashion" is forcing planners to reshape the way they think about the role of town planning (Wenban-Smith, 1986, p. 19). Despite the best efforts of town planners, English cities and towns experience urban sprawl, unwanted commercial development, environmental damage, vacant land in inner city areas, and the destruction of urban communities through slum clearance and redevelopment. Indeed, the English planning system can no longer be considered a "rational model of forward planning" (see Wenban-Smith, 1986, p. 27). This realization is one of the primary motivations for pushing local planning toward the more flexible systems discussed in Chapter 3.

One of the most important limitations of town planners is their inability to forecast trends accurately. Predicting future growth and land-use has been problematic and of little value. Few planners, economists or urban geographers predicted the rapid decline of central cities in the United States and Europe or the impact computers would have in the 1980s and 1990s. Technological change has allowed modern small companies to compete with large manufacturers and may be responsible for the growing influence of small businesses in advanced economies. Similarly, telecommunications technologies have allowed for stunning job growth in the services sector. The impact on urban economic growth and land development has been startling. Increasingly employment is decentralizing to the places where people live (Garreau, 1991) while manufacturing technologies have shifted to sprawling single story complexes in rural and semi-rural areas.

In the United States, one of the most time-consuming activities of local planners occurs over rezonings. There are even application procedures and fee schedules designed specifically for amending zoning laws. Despite the fact that zoning maps were developed as static blueprints for development, rezonings take up more time among local planners than virtually any other planning activity. "The frequency of rezoning requests," notes one expert, "is created largely by the difficulty of predicting land uses (Kelly, 1988, p. 253). Local planners are not able to effectively forecast the demand for particular sites as their cities evolve.

The inability to forecast future development accurately creates significant problems for local communities wishing to encourage economic development. In Florida, as mentioned earlier, communities desiring development have to demonstrate that their existing infrastructure can support such new development. This requires communities to build roads, sewers, water systems, etc. before development, even though patterns may not be well established. Ironically, these rules place poorer communities at a significant disadvantage since they cannot afford to build new infrastructure without the support of new development.

The inability of town planners to predict the pace, pattern, and nature of future growth is not unique to local planning attempts. National planning too has had limited success. The British experience was sufficiently poor that continued economic decline in the 1950s, 1960s and 1970s, resulted in over twelve years of conservative rule, beginning with the election of free-market conservative Margaret Thatcher in 1979. Singapore's attempt to stimulate a high-tech manufacturing revolution also failed to launch its economy into the post-industrial economic era. Even the much vaunted MITI in Japan has experienced significant forecasting errors. The Ministry attempted unsuccessfully (fortunately) to discourage Sony from entering into the electronics market and Honda from entering automobile production. In the case of Honda, MITI felt that the top auto producers already in existence in Japan were sufficient to fill existing automotive demand. Resistance from MITI was in part responsible for Honda's investment in the United States market.

Another important flaw in the modern system of town planning is the institutionalization of rent seeking behaviour. Rent seeking occurs when private parties use the political system to gain economic advantage. Extensive town planning systems essentially politicize the land development process, allowing individuals to exert influence over the pace and pattern of development as well as the distribution of rewards. In the United States, private interests have continually used the planning process to profit from new development (Hall, 1989), leading many planning critics to question its ability to fulfil a public mission.

The British experience also suggests that, despite the public spirited and utopian origin of European town planning, private interests are able to use the planning system to gain advantage over others. In the Oxford case study, for example, local planners negotiated with developers to include space in their new development for local firms. An architectural firm agreed initially to occupy the space. Unlike in cases of market exchanges, in order to secure the space the architectural firm merely had to ensure that it was in a better bargaining position than other local firms with respect to the planning process. The likelihood of an accounting firm specializing in private professional services having the same type of access to the planning system as an architectural firm integrally connected to the system is low. By restricting who could occupy the space and micro-managing land development, the commercial office market was effectively removed from the accountability inherent in economic markets.

A third drawback to contemporary town planning methods is its inability to achieve comprehensiveness in town plans or to fully comprehend the complexity of communities. An increasingly vocal debate is emerging within the planning literature, questioning the principles and practice of modern town planning. "The future of Town Planning," notes one practitioner, "depends on the identification of a philosophical basis to replace the worn out rational/hierarchical/ comprehensive/bureaucratic set of ideas behind the empty husk of the present system." (Wenban-Smith, 1986, p. 28)

Ironically, a glance at the experience of the United States shows a substantial retreat from the comprehensive planning doctrine that hinged on detailed zoning classifications. While zoning has achieved some of the aims of its creators — such as separating uses considered incompatible by professional planners and subordinating private interests to public interests (re: planners) — its has been far less successful at producing high-quality working and living conditions or addressing regional economic problems (Haar and Kayden, 1989).

Even within the criticism of planning within the profession, however, inconsistencies abound that complicate prospects for reforming contemporary approaches and providing a more realistic foundation for town planning. Disaffection with traditional planning has led a crop of "neotraditionalists" who yearn for the urban structure of older, smaller historical cities (Knack, 1989). Capitalizing on ideas from European architects, neotraditionalists argue that the emphasis on detailed separation of uses through zoning and low density development has created a sterile urban environment. In its place, they argue for smaller communities, mixed uses and grid-like transportation systems to facilitate movement within the community. In a large part, the new vision attempts to create congestion in order to promote activity in public places.

Even the neotraditionalists are reluctant to let development occur according to the dictates of the market. In fact, the code for the neotraditionalist towns reflects a substitution of utopian visions about urban life and cities. The founders, for example, created a set of "urban standards" that specify how much land should be left for greenbelts and civic purposes, width of streets, curb radius, window types, roof overhangs, materials to be used in construction, etc. Indeed, while ostensibly building on the failures of existing town planning schemes, the neotraditionalist vision may be substituting an even more rigid system in its place.

The current methods of town planning are simply inconsistent with the way the world works. Effective town planning requires that long-term goals can be achieved, that all relevant information about the nature of existing development is known, that change is predictable and that human behaviour can be moulded to fit the visions of town planners. Successful town planning requires the absence of uncertainty. In fact, one of the principle arguments for town planning is its ability to reduce uncertainty and provide an effective mechanism for achieving socially agreed upon end goals. Instead, town planners have been frustrated by market-driven activity inconsistent with approved plans, and often lament the tendency of local planners to modify them.

Moreover, the tools of the planners' trade are inconsistent with the ultimate goals of planning. In practice, town planning is reactive rather than pro-active. Planners can influence, but not control, property markets and developers. Since they are incapable of knowing what private markets will do at any given time, planners are forced to respond to developers in property markets. Moreover, even when planners are able to influence particular development projects or sites, they may be forced to bow to public pressure through referenda or local politicians. As a result, planners do not plan development, even though their tools presume that they do (see the discussion in Peiser, 1990; Garreau, 1991).

Of course, at least in principle, planning would have an important advantage over private markets if communities could agree on common goals and a general willingness to allocate resources in ways that would achieve those goals. Indeed, much of the enthusiasm for town planning resulted from the apparent effectiveness of planners to allocate resources efficiently and productively during World War II. Unfortunately for town planning, few goals are achieved through consensus, and the public interest is difficult to define, let alone interpret. Often, planning is done without public participation. Indeed, in many cases, including that of Hong Kong, public participation is not required and occurs at the discretion of the planners involved in granting planning permission. In the United States, the public can reject planning decisions through referenda, but there is evidence of the erosion of public participation here as well.

In conclusion, the words of urban planner Lloyd Rodwin should serve as a sobering warning to those enamoured with the potential of town planning to create a better society:

> In short, it does not take great insight today to see that, however inadequate the market may be, there is no reason to suppose that urban planners will necessarily do a better job, at least in the short or intermediate term. This reality of the inadequacy of planners and their tools offsets the other reality of the inadequacies of the market and price mechanism. (Rodwin, 1981, p. 230)

Two Approaches to Urban Development

The apparent failure of town planning to achieve its goals and its inherently political nature have important implications for modern town planning, particularly for cities that wish to promote healthy economies. Cities and nations are faced with two approaches to urban development. One approach, reflecting the modern planner's world view, sees the market as a chaotic process driven by narrow private interests that obscures or ignores the public interest. Intervention is required to correct the market mechanism and ensure that resources are allocated efficiently to produce a productive, mutually supportive quality of life.

The other perspective views the market as generally self-correcting. The price system, by catering to the narrow self-interests of producers and consumers, provides accountability by ensuring the supplier produces what consumers want. If a developer builds Class B office space, while consumers prefer Class A, the developer will have difficulty leasing his space and may, in fact, go out of business. Similarly, if a residential developer builds middle-income flats, but the market requires low-income flats, he or she will be forced to reduce the price on the flats to make them affordable, or go out of business.

Some planners have suggested that planning and market systems should be integrated (Wenban-Smith, 1986; Healy, 1992). Yet, the two systems are based on two fundamentally different premises with dramatically different implications for public policy. Contemporary town planning is, by necessity, bureaucratic and dictatorial. Planners, effectively, attempt to determine the pace and pattern of land development, imposing rules and standards they believe are most consistent with their vision of the public interest or public purpose. In effect, only planners need to actively participate in the planning process and developers exist merely to carry out the requirements of the plan.

Market-driven development, in contrast, is decentralized and democratic. Market transactions do not take place unless two parties voluntarily agree to an exchange of goods that each values.

Economic markets are driven by expectations about the willingness of the other party in the transaction to participate, to value the product highly enough to spend his or her income on the product (whether it be an office or residential flat) and improve the quality of his or her life. Similar requirements for voluntary participation are not required (or desired) in conventional town planning since, in principle, appropriate uses can be determined objectively and independently of the desires of residents, employers, and local developers, all of whom are participants in market-driven property development.

Implications for Town Planning in Hong Kong

As Hong Kong's move towards an accountable government is completed, public administration will become even further politicized. While the publicly visible features of Western democracies may have been less evident in the past (e.g., public demonstrations, vocal opposition to existing policy), the influence of interest groups in the policy-making and implementation process has long been recognized (Harris, 1988). These groups have been able to influence government to serve their interests within the administrative structure of the Hong Kong government.

While Hong Kong is unlikely to adopt the features of public participation evident in more contentious Western democracies (Kuan and Lau, 1989), several features of the emerging system will enhance the effectiveness of interest groups in the political process. Since functional constituencies will control at least half of the members of LegCo, the political system has ensured that interest groups will have an institutionalized voice in the political process. Thus, the process of interest-group politics that has evolved in Western democracies largely outside the formal framework of government has been formally incorporated into Hong Kong's policy-making process. As political inhibitions against social and economic intervention further weaken, the opportunity for special interest groups to intervene in the policy making stage will increase. The result will be open and intensive lobbying by special interest groups to influence public policy outcomes. The results of these changes could have important impacts on economic growth and development.[2]

The politicization of public administration will affect the planning process as well. The recommendation that the planning apparatus expand citizen participation in the plan making and land development process is in part a reflection of this move toward a more open political process. Moreover, Hong Kong's public servants are likely to take on more activist roles within their own departments. The separation of administration and policy will break down as the bureaucracy becomes even more sensitive to the demands of its "clients."[3]

In Western industrialized countries, these effects are most commonly seen in active lobbying of state legislatures for special interest legislation. On the local level, as the previous discussions highlighted, planning and zoning decisions often reflect the narrow political interests of existing residents. In some cases, the effect of this politicized process is to significantly constrain land development by lengthening the development process and restricting the availability of land.

An inevitable outcome of the planning reforms in Hong Kong will be an increase in uncertainty through the politicization of planning procedures. The current proposals provide for more discretion on the part of planners and a significantly enhanced role for the public in both plan making and plan application processes. As the planning system continues to open itself to public discussion and debate, land development will experience delays through the development

---

2. The pioneering work on interest groups and economic growth is Olson (1982). See also North (1987).

3. The importance of politics in public administration has been particularly evident in the American system. In the course of administering programmes, public servants also become policy makers by using their background, experience, and values to determine how programmes should be implemented and what aspects of the programme should be given priority. An excellent review of these trends in the American system can be found in Mosher (1990). The Hong Kong system of public administration is likely to incorporate many of the same featues as the political system becomes more open, fragmented and representative.

approval process as well as the plan making and modification process. The extent to which these changes will disrupt the current system and impact the Hong Kong economy is the focus of the remaining chapters.

The resilience of the system is surprising, given the attempts by professional planners to reform and upgrade local planning and zoning ordinances. Moreover, most professional planners in Hong Kong conform to conventional beliefs about the role of planning and zoning in controlling land-use. Planners in most industrialized countries, for example, consider mixed uses of commercial and residential property inefficient. Similarly, many Hong Kong planners have argued that the juxtaposition of industrial and residential areas, or the location of certain types of facilities such as auto repair shops on the lower floors of apartment buildings, is inappropriate and inefficient. To protect the interests of the public, according to planners, intervention in land use is essential.

Will Hong Kong planners be more successful than their Western counterparts in managing economic growth? Given the reforms outlined in the Consultative Document, the results are likely to be disappointing and may inadvertently compromise Hong Kong's competitiveness. In a large part, this is a result of the incompatibility between economic growth and change and current planning principles.

CHAPTER 5

Town Planning in Hong Kong

Hong Kong's planning department has the same goals as planning departments throughout the industrialized world. Most professional planners in Hong Kong, and their proposed reforms, bear important similarities in philosophy and content to systems in other countries. In fact, many Hong Kong planners have been trained and educated at many of the most prestigious planning schools in the United States and United Kingdom.

The importance of conventional planning theory and Western legal institutions is evident in the laws defining the scope and responsibilities of town planning in Hong Kong and in the official documents prepared by the Planning Department. Current planning practice in Hong Kong is grounded in the 1939 *Town Planning Ordinance* which permits the Governor-in-Council, with the advice of the Town Planning Board, to "promote the health, safety, convenience and general welfare of the community by making provision for the systematic preparation and approval of plans for the future lay-out of existing and potential urban areas as well as the types of building suitable for erection therein." A publication developed by the Planning Department describes planning as "the process of guiding and controlling the development and use of land, with the aim of promoting the health, safety, convenience and general welfare of the community." Its role, the brochure continues, is to balance the competing interests of housing, commerce, industry, and other community interests in the struggle for scarce land.

Moreover, in the introduction to the *Comprehensive Review of Town Planning Ordinance*, the Consultative Document describes planning as an attempt "to promote the right development in the right place and at the right time, so as to bring about a better organized, more efficient and more pleasant place in which to live and to work." The planner's mission requires assessing the "requirements for and designation of land for all types of uses ...." These statements would be at home in any standard textbook on planning and land-use in Western countries such as the United States or United Kingdom.

What distinguishes Hong Kong planners from Western planners, however, is not the ultimate goals or intent of local planning ordinances. Rather, Hong Kong planners have traditionally been much less aggressive than their colleagues in the West, carefully avoiding controls or regulation that might hinder economic growth (see Bristow 1984). Planning activism has been limited to development control specifications built into leases auctioned by the government or general guidelines specified in *Outline Zoning Plans* (OZPs) developed by the local planning department. The passive nature of the Hong Kong planning system, however, may be changing as town planners attempt to come to grips with the rapid political and economic changes that have been occurring in the territory since the 1960s.

Planning Activism in Hong Kong

In Hong Kong, planners have become increasingly active in the planning process. As in the United States, much of this activism has come through heightened concerns for the environment. For example, some claim a "casualty" of economic growth has been the environment.[1] Extensive pollution in Victoria and Tolo Harbours has raised important questions concerning the viability of the environment when industrial waste is dumped haphazardly and untreated by local industries. Unfortunately, attempts to regulate environmental damage have been largely unsuccessful and disappointing (Siddall, 1991), especially since many existing factories have been exempted from meeting the new, stricter requirements.

---

1. A review of environment issues in Hong Kong and the world can be found in Kwong (1990).

Environmental Planning

Nevertheless, the government has been active in its attempts to address environmental issues through tax policy as well as land-use regulation. Concerns over environmental damage, for example, led to a reduction in plot ratios in the old industrial area of Kwai Chung (Yeh, 1991, p. 25). While this may be viewed as an isolated incident, concern over air and noise pollution has put additional pressures on authorities to control development more tightly. Thus, the Consultative Document specifically points to the need for environmental impact statements to accompany new applications for development in environmentally sensitive areas. Interest groups have already emerged to intercede in the policy making process for political reasons. The local chapter of the environmental group Friends of the Earth challenged the government's recent plans to sell 30 hectares of public park land to developers attempting to build a resort of over 300 homes and an 18-hole golf course. Friends of the Earth argued that the golf course was an example of "creeping urbanization" and the valley should remain "unspoilt" ("What We are Fighting For", 1991). The development was halted after a judicial challenge that argued the public was improperly consulted in the development process.

Similarly, concern over congestion resulted in downgrading residential developments in the mid-levels on Hong Kong Island (Yeh, 1991, p. 25). Public officials and planners questioned whether the existing infrastructure — roads, water, sewers, etc. — could handle more intensive residential development. Some officials have specifically highlighted the inability of emergency vehicles to climb the narrow roads into the mid-levels during rush hour. Similar worries over land-use incompatibility and the suitability of existing infrastructure contributed to the decisions to downgrade the development potential of industrial districts such as Tsuen Wan and Kwai Chung.

The New Towns

Hong Kong, in fact, has practical experience with complex town planning schemes. Beginning in the mid-1950s, British, American, and Hong Kong planners have been integrally involved in developing New Towns as a way to decentralize the territory's growing population and burgeoning industry. Population densities in Hong Kong are some of the greatest in the world (Fig. 5.1). Within the metropolitan area, Hong Kong's population densities exceed those of other populous cities by wide margins. Moreover, particular districts of Hong Kong have extraordinarily high densities. Mong Kok is the most densely populated, with over 170,000 people per square kilometer in 1981. While these densities fell to slightly under 120,000 people per square kilometer in 1991, Mong Kok remains one of the most densely populated areas of the world.

The New Towns are credited as an essential intervention that compensated for the inability of the private market to respond adequately to Hong Kong's rising population and demand for quality, affordable housing (see Bristow, 1989; Gallion and Eisner, 1986, pp. 120–24). Thus, the Hong Kong government initiated the New Towns to reduce population densities to more acceptable levels. Over

Figure 5.1: Population Densities in Hong Kong and Selected World Cities

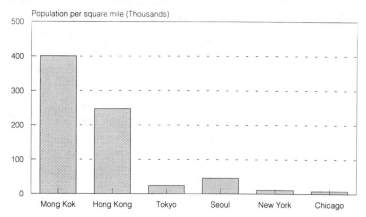

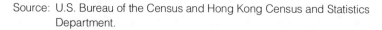

Source: U.S. Bureau of the Census and Hong Kong Census and Statistics Department.

the past four decades, Hong Kong has sponsored comprehensive New Town Development in Kwun Tong, Tuen Mun, Sha Tin, Yuen Long, Tai Po, Junk Bay, Tin Shui Wai, and Sheung Shui (Fig. 5.2).

While the territory's overall population density has increased from 4,870 people per square kilometer in 1981 to 5,385 in 1991, most districts in the built-up areas of Kowloon experienced declines. The bulk of the territory's rising population appears to have been absorbed by the New Territories and new developments along the Eastern and Southern regions of Hong Kong Island (Fig. 5.3).

The New Towns were intended to do far more than simply move people out of the central city cores. They were expected to be self-contained and balanced communities as well. In fact, planners' visions have been uncharacteristically ambitious in using the New Towns as a mechanism for implementing sophisticated town planning concepts to create new cities that would be effectively self-sufficient. The ambitions of the town planners in the first phase of the New Towns is represented by the explanatory statement accompanying the OZP for Tuen Mun, one of the first generation of New Towns:

Figure 5.2: Population Densities by District, 1991

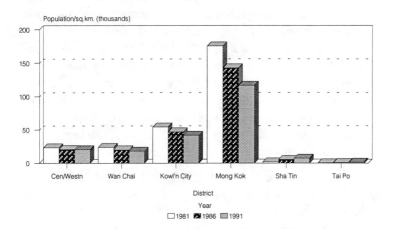

Source: Hong Kong Census and Statistics Department.

Figure 5.3: Population Densities, 1991

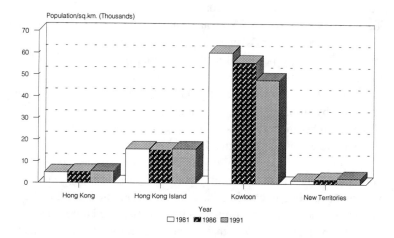

Source: Hong Kong Census and Statistics Department.

The planning of a new town presents a unique opportunity to design a total environment .... The structure of a new town is predetermined by general planning principles and land use allocation in accordance with the adopted planning standards. The form and character are then derived from the interpretation of this policy decision in building forms. The physical elements which make up the environment ... must be well related to provide a visual sense of coherence. Viewed from a distance, the new town should present the impression of a tapestry of urban forms amid green foliages. However within this overall design there should be room for drama and contrast. The planning objectives must be to give visual pleasure, a sense of identity and the civic pride to the people of the town. (quoted in Bristow, 1989, pp. 176–77)

The success of the New Towns in achieving many of these goals has been limited (see Bristow, 1989, pp. 277–311). While population has become more decentralized, the New Towns have failed to attract industry and substantial private housing. Indeed, much of the population in the New Towns live in public housing. According to Hong

Kong's planning department, the number of persons living in public housing is greater than the number in private housing in seven of the eight New Towns. In Tsuen Wan, the largest new town, 426,000 people live in public housing compared to only 272,000 in private housing. In Sha Tin, 424,000 people live in public housing while another 243,000 live in private housing. Only in Yuen Long does the number of people in private housing (87,000) exceed those in public housing (61,000). To some extent, the decentralization in population is as much through private development centered around Hong Kong Island and Kowloon as the development of new residential flats outside of congested areas. Planning in Hong Kong, like planning in other countries, is still subject to the vagaries of market processes in land development.

Observers note that many of the failures of the New Towns center on the inability of planners to adequately forecast demographic and economic trends. Government policy, particularly planning policy, has been reactive, rather than pro-active. Roger Bristow, one of the foremost experts on town planning in Hong Kong, notes that "reactive planning largely accounts for the fact that the nature and form of the Hong Kong new towns are born out of short-term thinking and policy-making with limited horizons" (1989, p. 307). In such an environment, the success of any long-term planning project will likely be compromised.

Thus, despite the worldwide attention Hong Kong has received because of its New Town developments, experience does not suggest that either town planning or planners will be much more successful if given yet more control over development.

Metroplan

The single largest justification for increased intervention in local development may come from the belief that a more complex economy requires a more sophisticated (and manipulative) town planning system. The most ambitious manifestation of the new planning activism may be represented by the Port and Airport Development Strategy (PADS) and Metroplan which, according to the Foreword to

Metroplan: The Selective Strategy written by Graham Barnes, former Secretary for Planning, Environment and Lands, provides "a framework which will guide the selection of projects and the priority given to them, so as to restructure and develop the city in a cost-effective way." Among Metroplan's basic principles are the thinning out of congested urban areas, encouraging growth beyond existing urbanized areas, planning the location, scale and timing of commercial development, and developing the new airport at Chek Lap Kok.

The government officials and planners initially outlined three different strategies for public comment. Each option included land-use plans based on projected populations, employment and land development. Through the process of public comment and discussion, a final hybrid version was created that is now a comprehensive guide to development in the Hong Kong metropolitan area. Metroplan includes detailed specifications of design standards (guiding principles), density guidelines, green space, and patterns of land uses. While not site specific, and intentionally broad, the plan is laying the general framework for comprehensive development control within the built-up areas of Hong Kong Island and Kowloon and inner New Towns.

To a large extent, however, Metroplan is a response to the huge infrastructure investments that are part of PADS. The government will be reclaiming hundreds of hectares of land, constructing a new airport, developing new rail and highway links, and extending existing sewer and water systems. Given these infrastructure investments, formal planning is an important element in the development process.

On the other hand, Metroplan includes attempts to control the pace and pattern of private development. Among the six broad aims of Metroplan are an attempt to "achieve a more balanced distribution of jobs relative to population concentrations, the locational preferences of new enterprises and the ease of travel" and to "rationalize land-use pattern to create a more acceptable urban environment" (pp. 19–21). Development controls will be used to manage development according to performance standards such as the number of jobs within the radii of railway stations, criteria for job/worker balance, degree of conformity to New Town standards and comprehensive redevelopment schemes. In many cases, performance criteria will be determined by the professional judgement of government officials.

The treatment of density controls may be one of the best indicators of how Metroplan intends to use land-use planning to manage growth. "It is evident," the government claims in *The Selective Strategy*, "that development densities must be planned to ensure that the volume of activities generated within each development zone and the capacities of transport systems, utilities and community facilities can function efficiently" (p. 53). Densities will be controlled by maximizing densities close to high capacity transport systems through planning and zoning, limiting densities in areas not served by high capacity transport, reducing densities in congested districts, and limiting densities in areas where visual impact is "of prime concern."

Imbedded in the guidelines and goals of Metroplan is a belief that market allocations of land are inherently flawed. Comprehensive planning must be used to ensure market-driven development does not abrogate objective standards set by planners concerning acceptable living and working conditions. Overall, Metroplan will serve as a policy instrument that will give town planners the flexibility they need to implement their land-use polices. In this respect, Metroplan represents state-of-the-art planning by using planning to set general guidelines and criteria for development. In this vein, Metroplan acknowledges that planning can do little to alter the general pattern of land development, but its impact on specific characteristics can be significant and important. Nevertheless, the plan also acknowledges that it is attempting to use planning to achieve an "optimal end-state" (p. 14). Toward this goal, government officials and planners will marshal the necessary financial resources to mount an aggressive campaign to redesign and shape metropolitan Hong Kong.

Future Directions in Town Planning

Even before the creation of current proposals for reform in the *Comprehensive Review*, planners in Hong Kong were anticipating a substantial increase in planning-related activity. After the "action planning" of the 1970s, notes a government publication in 1988, "the planning profession in Hong Kong is now about to launch into a new era when the Government re-orients planning activity and funds in the development and redevelopment of the Main Urban Areas" (Office of Town Planning, p. 17). Much of the new activism surrounds the complexities of modern economic growth. The push toward financial services, the decline of light manufacturing, the new airport and container terminal, and the rising prominence of information technologies are requiring planners to make "hard choices on the allocation of limited resources to support many differing needs" (Taylor and Kwok, 1989, p. 319). Planners increasingly see their role as that of a manager of the territory's resources. "Diverse demands," observe urban planners Bruce Taylor and Yin-wan Kwok, "have forced Hong Kong's planners to adopt an increasingly forward-looking posture." (ibid.)

These ambitions are being encouraged by researchers who perceive an important role for planners in shaping and directing future economic development. The non-profit Hong Kong Industrial Estates Corporation was founded in 1977 to create industrial parks to "broaden the industrial base and upgrade the technological level of industry" (Y. P. Ho, 1992, p. 209). The industrial estates would provide land for land-intensive industries such as many new high technology industries. The purpose of the organization is to provide cheap land through land-use policies that encourage the establishment of "new industries of long-term importance to Hong Kong's industrial development" (ibid). Yet, as mentioned in Chapter 2, this may be a misguided strategy given the restructuring of the economy and the apparent comparative advantage of Guangdong and Shenzhen.

The tools planners will use to fulfil the new, more active mission are taken primarily from the conventional planners' toolbox found in most Western countries. By extending planning authority and development controls, planners can place limits on new development to ensure that property markets account for social needs. Thus, planners argue that more detailed zoning regulations, density controls, set-back requirements and other development controls will be necessary to protect the quality of life of Hong Kong residents. Moreover, the Consultative Document argues that development control should be linked to building applications and permits, forcing the private sector to consult local planners before they begin projects. This link, through a device called a planning certificate, would formally establish the local planning authority as the final arbitor in development.

Whether Hong Kong planners will be more successful in achieving their goals is a matter of substantial debate and discussion. But, given the nature of land development in Hong Kong, concerns over maintaining a healthy economy, and the tools used in controlling development, the results are likely to be disappointing.

The Leasehold System

Another distinguishing feature of the Hong Kong planning system, aside from the historically passive nature of planning, is its political context. Virtually all land in Hong Kong is legally owned and managed by the Crown, i.e. the government. Hong Kong Island and the Kowloon Peninsula were ceded to Britain in 1842 and 1860 respectively. The New Territories were "leased" by treaty to Britain on a 99-year lease in 1898. Private parties purchase leases for the land, but legal ownership and control remains in the hands of government. This contrasts sharply with the case of the United States, where developable land is almost entirely owned on a free-hold basis (complete private ownership), and England, where land is owned on leasehold and free-hold basis.

Private developers and land "owners" gain use of the land by purchasing leases issued by the government, most often (but not exclusively) at public auction. Land is almost always auctioned off at prices higher than the government's minimum, or reserve, price. These prices, it should be noted, are sustained by the expectation that the land can be developed to its fullest potential given existing planning restrictions and the state of the market. Thus, unlike the situation in England and the United States, where land sells below its development potential, Hong Kong's property markets typically value land at prices reflecting maximum development potential.

Contemporary leases sold at auction include a variety of restrictions, or lease conditions. To promote the "optimum use of land as well as to control the development in order that the environment is not adversely affected", lease conditions often contain restrictions that specify site coverage, plot ratio, building height, and minimum floor area to be constructed (Office of Town Planning, 1988, p. 29). Lease conditions have become increasingly complex in recent years as planners have incorporated more development controls to mitigate the apparent willingness of private developers to disregard the public interest. Leases, then, increasingly include development controls common in the development and zoning plans of many Western countries.

Thus, even though the Hong Kong government has a reputation for being non-interventionist in economic affairs and formal town planning, it has been thoroughly enmeshed in land-use planning and development through the leasehold system since the earliest days of the colony. Some argue that the planning policy in Hong Kong consisted of "non-planning" or non-interventionism in its control of leases until the late 1950s. Technically, this relationship between landowners and the government dispenses with many of the "messy" legal problems associated with controlling land-uses found in countries with more decentralized systems based on freehold ownership such as the United States.[2] Since the government owns the land, it may have a legal (and perhaps an ethical) obligation to supervise and define broadly conceived uses of land in the public interest. In this context, despite a historical commitment to allow a largely free evolution of land-use, government intervention into land development may be more easily justifiable if it pursues a more interventionist approach to planning. In this context, assessing the impacts of planning, and the role of planners, may be even more important in Hong Kong than in other countries.

The leasehold system and the nature of planning in Hong Kong has created a truly unique system of land-use and development control. One of its most provocative features may be the relationship

---

2. This interpretation differs from that of others who have written on this subject, most notably Yeh (1992, pp. 24–27).

between leaseholders and the government. For property developers, leases are considered a "contract" (although not a legally enforceable one) between the government and the owner of the lease.[3] The lease is purchased with full knowledge of the restrictions on development (through lease conditions or statutory land-use plans) with the understanding that the land will be developed to the maximum level permitted. Developers, then, view the sale of the lease as implicit permission to fully develop the land, and therefore they bid on prices in public auction (or pay land premia for redevelopment) accordingly.

The informal contractual nature of land development is not purely abstract and theoretical. Since leases are purchased with the intention of developing land, and land premia and bids are based on the full development value of the land, developers have viewed the lease purchase (for virgin land) as the "point of commitment" for development between the government and property developers. Similarly, a private individual purchases a lease from another private individual with the expectation of assuming the conditions of the lease and the right to develop the land in accordance with the lease's stipulations (and existing zoning plans). Despite the absence of a formal contract allowing maximum development, the system of land development operates as if these formal arrangements existed and were respected by all parties involved in the contract (especially the government, which exacts land premia based on the value of the anticipated development).

On a practical level, the lease has been interpreted as a "development right" for its purchasers. For instance, when the lease is sold, the government has implicitly given the developer the right to develop the land to the fullest limit of the lease. Thus, when developers bid on new leases, they tender their bids based on the expectation that they will be able to fully develop the property. Hence, the lease is interpreted as an implicit contract between the government and developer.

Moreover, procedures exist for developers to modify the lease or

---

3. This interpretation is based on extensive interviews conducted by the author with developers in Hong Kong as well as with local planners.

change the land-use requirements specified in the lease. If the change results in increasing the value of the property (or its development potential) the developer "compensates" the government by paying a "premium" on the land.

It is significant that, as government officials and local planners emphasize, this is not a legal point of commitment, or a legal contract between the government and property developers specifying the extent of development control over land use. Rather, this interpretation of the role and rights of leaseholders has emerged as a product of the evolution and practice of planning and land-use control in Hong Kong. From an economic perspective, significant changes to informal rules that "govern" or regulate property markets can be as important as formal or legal rules. Similar informal rules exist in virtually all planning systems and may, in fact, be as significant in the development process as formal rules and procedures (see Thomas, *et al.*, 1983).

While not legally binding (at least with respect to planning and development control), many developers believe this element of the leasehold system has been the cornerstone of property development in Hong Kong, allowing land markets to work efficiently and effectively to meet the changing demands of consumers and producers in the local economy. The existence of this implicit contract has been instrumental in reducing uncertainty within property markets because, historically, the government has been reluctant to alter the development potential of land stipulated through the lease conditions or changes in zoning plans.

In sum, the contractual nature of land development in Hong Kong is a by-product of its leasehold system. Since the government specifies conditions for development in the leases when they are auctioned, and collects land premia from developers when they request permission to develop land more intensely, the development permission process creates an informal contract between the two parties. This contractual nature of development has become an important informal institution that has produced stability in land development, encouraging investment in Hong Kong. The formal rules and procedures that govern land development builds on this informal relationship between developers and the government of Hong Kong.

Planning Practice in Hong Kong

Land-use control and development in Hong Kong has evolved over several decades in the absence of the detailed, formal rules and procedures found in most other planning systems although procedures and guidelines are published by local planners and administrative agencies. The fact that of these formal rules do not exist has required the development community and local planners to create informal rules that have allowed the system to work smoothly and provide substantial certainty in the development process. The evolutionary nature of planning and land-use development has also helped reduce uncertainty in the development process, encouraging property investment.

For example, leases sold at public auction have included restrictions on land uses that conform to existing zoning plans. These restrictions have become more detailed over the years to provide more certainty to potential developers so they can calculate their bids. As long as the government honours the lease, a high degree of certainty is implicit in the development process even though the government is not legally or formally bound to the lease for planning purposes. This certainty allows developers to more carefully calculate future income from these developments, and increases the value of the property. "With the permitted development specified in the lease," notes Anthony Gar-on Yeh, "the private developers are willing to pay a higher price in land sales because of the certainty of the development potentials." (1991, p. 11) In other words, developers are willing to bid on the land based on its development potential without the vaguaries implicit in negotiating development permission in Western countries.

In keeping with the evolutionary nature of planning in Hong Kong, land-use regulation has rarely been influenced by radical change. The most recent change occurred when the *Town Planning Amendment Ordinance* was passed in 1991, allowing for more development control, particularly in the New Territories. Before the 1991 Amendment, the most important change to land-use regulations occurred in 1973 when the courts invalidated the government's power to use notes developed by the Office of Town Planning on zoning plans as guidelines for development. Legislation was passed in 1974 to give statutory authority to these notes. This amendment, however, represented an attempt to codify existing practice into law and did not represent a significant break with the administration of planning in Hong Kong (Bristow, 1984, pp. 127–29). Prior to this, the *Buildings Ordinance of 1955* gave the government the power to refuse permission to approve planning applications that were inconsistent with official zoning plans.

Reforms proposed in the 1980s and 1990s, particularly those outlined in the Consultative Document, attempt to complete the evolution of town planning along lines common in other countries, particularly the United Kingdom. Planners want to formally link development permission to the approval of building permits, a practice common in the Netherlands and the United States. Interestingly, these links were formally adopted in the early twentieth century in these countries as part of their push toward more comprehensive town planning.

Planning in Hong Kong currently covers a wide range of issues and occurs on three levels: territorial, sub-regional, and local. Territorial planning provides broad guidelines for local development with respect to transportation and land-use, although the rapid development of the territory in the post-war era has required substantial flexibility on the part of local planners. Sub-regional planning is intended to transform "territory-wide goals into sub-regional objectives" by linking territorial development strategies to local plans that provide the substantive framework and guidelines for development control by local planning authorities (Office of Town Planning, 1988, p. 23).

On the local, or district, level, planning has taken the form of preparing OZPs that provide the general guidelines for development in specified areas by designating general land uses and major road systems. Planning authority through OZPs was extended to the New Territories through the 1991 Amendment. Development Permission Areas (DPA), another product of the 1991 amendment, are transitional plans prepared to control development during the process of amending OZPs.

Generally, land uses are categorized based on whether they are residential, commercial, industrial, government-institutional-community, open space, green belt or special use. In addition to the general categories of uses, a schedule of notes is attached to OZPs that restrict land-use by categorizing uses as either Column One or Column Two. Column One uses are permitted at any time.[4] If, for example, the OZP for a residential area allows a swimming pool under Column One, the developer is not required to obtain permission for that type of development from the Town Planning Board. If the developer is interested in putting in a retail shop that is specified as a Column Two use in the development, he must ask the Town Planning Board for permission to incorporate it into the development. It is important to be aware that Column Two uses are almost always approved by the Town Planning Board.

The current local planning system has two phases: plan making and plan application. The plan making process entails the preparation and implementation of statutory plans regulating the layout for particular areas. The responsibility for drawing up OZPs and DPAs rests with the Town Planning Board although all plans are legally initiated and approved by the Governor-in-Council. Once the statutory plan is considered "suitable" for publication by the Town Planning Board, it is exhibited for public inspection and comment for two months. The statutory plan becomes effective immediately upon its publication after the Governor-in-Council approves the plan.

Under the current system, draft plans are subject to an objection process before the plan is sent to the Governor for approval and publication. The objection procedure is primarily a mechanism for hearing public views on the new plan. The Town Planning Board can amend the plans to meet objections, but the plans must be exhibited for public inspection again. Currently there is no statutory time limit on hearing objections, and, according to the Consultative Document, "past experience has shown that [the objection process] can take up to

---

4. These are comparable to "always permissable uses" found in other countries.

two years or more to complete" (p. 20). This process has not disrupted property development because plan applications are not tied to OZPs when they are under review.

The plan application process applies to the actual process of developing land. Plan applications are currently used to ensure that development conforms to existing zoning and land-use restrictions as outlined in the OZP, explanatory statements and attached notes. The Town Planning Board must approve or reject an application within two months of its submission. Appeals of Town Planning Board decisions are made to the Board or through a petition to the Governor-in-Council. Currently there are few opportunities for the public to submit their views on plan applications, a perceived drawback to the current planning system.

Building plans can be rejected if they do not conform to the *Buildings Ordinance* which, in addition to leases, provides the principal mechanism for controlling development. The *Buildings Ordinance* allows the Town Planning Board to reject plan applications if they do not conform to a draft, approved, or master layout plan; they do not conform in design, height, type or intended use in the immediate neighbourhood or previously existing use; the buildings are used for residences and "dangerous trades"; or the buildings do not have adequate access to a public street. Control over development, however, cannot be exercised over redevelopment if a change in use does not occur.

By most accounts, even among those within the government, the system of land-use planning that exists in Hong Kong has worked well. Although problems exist, the system has provided broader latitude for development than developers possess in many other countries. In more decentralized planning systems that allow for extensive community input, specific developments must be approved individually by a zoning or planning board. Any deviations from the existing zoning plan (which can be very detailed) require the developer to apply for a zoning variance to allow for the proposed use. Nevertheless, some developers have argued that Hong Kong's system is still inflexible since there are some uses that are not permitted at all.

Problems with the Current Planning System

In recent years, planners have been frustrated in their attempts to use planning to control development. Indeed, one of the principal objectives of the reforms proposed in the Consultative Document is to broaden the enforcement and development control powers of the planning authorities. At the same time, planners have become more and more willing to intervene in the development process to direct or influence the pace and pattern of development. In some cases, these changes have been clear and open. The moratorium on development in Pokfulam and plot ratio reductions in the Mid-levels and Tsuen Wan serve as examples that will be discussed in more detail later (Chapter 6). In other areas, the changes will be less visible, as in the regulatory reforms suggested in the Consultative Document.

Yet, if adopted, the proposals are likely to have significant impacts on property markets if they increase uncertainty in the development process or weaken property rights. By injecting more variability into the plan making and plan application process, the reforms risk increasing uncertainty, since special interests and public administrators will have greater discretion over determining the types, pace, and pattern of development on the district level (see also Wiltshaw, 1986). To the extent that it can reduce uncertainty about future land-use, planning can hasten development or redevelopment (Neutze, 1987, p. 287; Titman, 1985). This is clearly evident in Hong Kong, where developers welcome lease restrictions because they increase certainty over permissable uses. To the extent that planning and planners increase uncertainty (e.g., by giving government officials more control over land development after leases are purchased and premia paid to the government), developers will be less inclined to invest in land development since future returns will be less certain. Unfortunately, the types of changes that the Consultative Document proposed will be likely to increase uncertainty in key areas of the development process.

The Consultative Document

Many of the features that are important to the smooth functioning of property markets are an anathema to town planners. Currently, development control exercised through the *Buildings Ordinance* and lease conditions effectively limits planning to the front-end of development. Planning changes that affect lease conditions require mutual consent of the leaser and the leasee, restricting the discretion of planners. If, for example, planners believed that the plot ratio for a residential area should be reduced to limit the impact of the development on congestion, the change would require the consent of both the developer and the government if the plot ratio was stipulated in the lease. The developer is unlikely to consent to such a change if it entails a financial loss.[5]

Yet, even critics of the leasehold planning system acknowledge that leases since the 1960s have accomplished many of the goals of planners. Unrestricted leases granted before World War II pose the most severe problems for planners since, according to the lease contract, virtually any type of development is allowed unless it contravenes the *Building Ordinance*. In some cases, leases were auctioned in the nineteenth century with only an expiration date (sometimes 999 years) and a right of automatic renewal.

This general lack of planning control, and the apparent conflict between market-driven property development and planning goals, led the Consultative Document to identify several areas for improvement in the existing planning system.

Lack of Comprehensive Planning Control

The lack of comprehensive planning control over development was identified as one of the overriding concerns of the Advisory Group. The *1939 Town Planning Ordinance*, the review observes, ignores many "contemporary" issues in modern planning such as environmental impact, civic design, conservation, and non-conforming uses. Enforcement through leases is extremely inflexible since planning

---

5. Consent would be more likely if the government were willing to compensate the developer for the financial loss due to the planning change.

requirements can only be imposed when the lease expires. And even when it does expire, planners may have little impact on future land-use if the lease includes a clause allowing for automatic renewal. These issues have become particularly important on Hong Kong Island and Kowloon where long term leases have few restrictions on land development (Yeh, 1991).

To ameliorate these problems, the proposals call for centralizing development control and enforcement in a Planning Authority. Through the use of a planning certificate, the Planning Authority would ensure that development conformed to existing OZPs before work even began. A planning certificate would be required even if the development consisted of Column One uses (even though, in principle, they are permitted at all times). The Planning Authority would also be permitted to stop work (or levy fines) on a construction site if the development were considered in violation of the existing plan or if a planning certificate had not been issued.

In concept and in practice, this reform represents a significant break with the past. The planning certificate can be used to require development to conform to plans that are in the draft and objection stages of consideration. The planning certificate would be issued after the public exhibition period for draft plans or, if an objection is raised on the site for development, after the objection review procedure (which could take up to nine months). The current system allows development to proceed as new drafts of statutory plans are being considered by the Town Planning Board. The planning certificate would be used to ensure that the developer complies with any draft or approved statutory plan or restrictions imposed by the planning board. By not issuing a planning certificate, planners could also prevent development if the site was under public objection, and ensure the development satisfied the Planning Authority's concerns over density, plot ratio, site coverage, etc.

While the reforms call for a statutory limit on the approval of the planning certificate approval process (60 days), a "developer would normally apply for a planning certificate before submission of detailed building plans to the Building Authority to ensure compliance with all planning requirements so as to avoid abortive work in the preparation of detailed building plans" (Consultative Document, p. 59). Discretionary power over density control and other planning-related provisions would be transferred to the Planning Authority from the Building Authority.

The introduction of the planning certificate entails a substantive shift in the development approval process from a system that emphasizes processing building applications to one that determines the suitability of development for planning purposes. The planning certificate will also give formal control over the development process to planners. Under the current system, planners exert informal control through their consultative role in the plan application process through the Buildings Department.

Compensation

A second issue identified, but not explicitly addressed in the recommendations, is compensation and betterment. Currently, the government is required to pay compensation to property owners only if their land is resumed for public purposes. In this case, compensation is determined by the "fair" market value of the land. Section 5 of The *Town Planning Ordinance* specifies that *no* compensation will be paid property owners for changes that occur through planning decisions. In principle, since the government is acting in the best interest of the public, changes in plans are not considered takings despite the fact that changes in land-use restrictions can have a dramatic impact on the value of developable lands. Thus, even if the planners decided to reduce plot ratios or restrict other types of development on property, legally these planning-oriented actions would not require the government to pay compensation even though they may be considered (by developers) as a breach in the implicit contract over the right to development land.

The compensation issue is complicated further by the fact that the government exacts land premia from developers who want to upgrade their land to capture the economic benefits of more intensive development. To maintain consistency, given the contractual nature of development in Hong Kong, the government should pay compensation to developers if the value of their property is downgraded through planning decisions. Even though the government is not legally required to pay compensation, economic development in Hong Kong hinges on the contractual nature of land development and the mutual respect implicit in that arrangement. If the government pursues planning objectives that significantly and negatively impact developer interests, uncertainty would be introduced into property markets with potentially significant economic and revenue-raising impacts.

Betterment, on the other hand, refers to planning actions that improve the value of property. In principle, public agencies (e.g., governments or planning agencies) make investments that enhance the value of property. These investments may be direct ones, such as investments in road networks, sewer systems, etc., or indirect ones, such as rezoning land to allow the development of a project with a higher return, or rezoning residential land to make it commercial, or allowing more intensive use of the land.

While the Consultative Document acknowledges the importance of these issues, the Advisory Group decided that the best course of action would be to refer compensation and betterment to a special committee to develop recommendations. These issues will be discussed in greater detail in Chapter 6.

Public Participation

The Consultative Document also identified the lack of public participation as a weakness of the current planning system. In order to ensure that the planning and development process more fully reflects the interests of the community, the review suggests that the planning process allow more public input at both the plan making and plan application stages. While the final decision still rests with the Governor-in-Council (avoiding direct public involvement through referenda on land development), opening the process will entail delays in the plan making and plan application processes.

A comparison of the current system with the proposed system shows more clearly the potential delays in the process. Technically, the proposed system suggests a framework that would allow the public to file objections to planning applications that could extend the approval process by three to nine months. The length of the delay would depend on whether the site exists in an area subject to a new draft plan (a new plan or revision of an old plan) and whether objections were raised on the site.

In the plan making stage, the proposed system would extend the plan exhibition period from two to three months (Fig. 5.4), allowing citizens more time to provide input into the planning process and raise objections to the proposed plan. This would in turn be followed by a period of consultation and evaluation that would in be followed by two more months of public exhibition. If objections were raised to the revised plan, a nine month period would be declared after which the plan could be either approved, refused, or approved with conditions.

Citizen participation in the plan making process is unlikely to be very disruptive unless it interferes with approvals of development applications.

Figure 5.4: The Plan Making Process

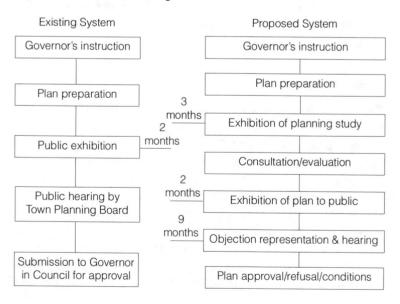

If the site were in an approved statutory plan area, the length of time needed to process the application would be three to four months, one to two months longer than the statutory time limit on planning applications under the current system (Fig. 5.5). If the planning application were rejected, the appeal procedures would add 21 days to notify the applicant of the rejection and three months for a review of the decision before the Planning Board. If the application were rejected again, the applicant would be able to appeal to an independent Appeals Board. Based on the timing and structure outlined in the Consultative Document, processing an application could easily take up to a year if it is subject to the appeals process.

If the site lay within an area subject to the plan exhibition or objection period, delays could be much longer. The planning application would be processed in the "usual" manner, but consideration by the planning board would be deferred until after the exhibition period or objection procedures were concluded. If objections were not

Figure 5.5: The Plan Application Process

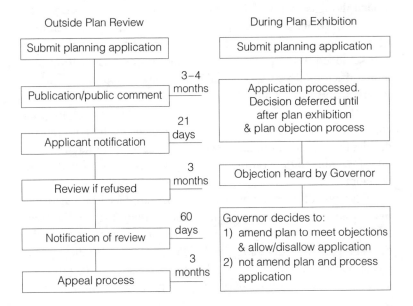

raised, the town planning board would consider the planning application after the two-month exhibition period. If objections were raised to the draft plan, the decision on the planning application would be deferred until after the objection process were concluded, a maximum of nine months after the expiration of the exhibition period. The process, of course, would be lengthened if the Governor-in-Council required more information before making a final decision.

Several other issues are raised in the Consultative Document, such as areas of special control, conservation, civic design, tree preservation, etc., but the principal parties affected by the proposed changes have not identified these issues as areas of major concern. This does not necessarily imply that the impacts of these changes would be insignificant, only that they fall outside the scope of the current study. These changes are unlikely to influence a significant fraction of development in Hong Kong.

Uncertainty and New Planning Procedures

The overriding concerns among Hong kong developers revolve around the uncertainty and increased risk that would be introduced into the development process as a result of the proposed reforms. Many believe that as the reforms are implemented, a random element will be added to the planning application process that will make it more difficult to forecast potential returns on development, dampening incentives for new investment in property markets. The introduction of a new system that ties development control to plan applications and the break-down of the contractual nature of property development would introduce uncertainty on several different levels, all of which could significantly impact economic growth and development.

One type of uncertainty that would be introduced into the planning system involves the *procedural uncertainty* that results from adopting a new planning framework. This uncertainty may be the easiest type to quantify since the design of the new planning system places boundaries on processing planning applications. The proposed system, for example, limits the planning application review process to between three and nine months by statute. The average length of the process, of course, depends on how often objections to new developments (or redevelopments) are raised. Nevertheless, the new system would increase the opportunity and likelihood that plan applications will result in a rejection or imposition of new, stricter conditions on development. Clearly, developments that are controversial and stir public sentiment would be subjected to longer application approvals than those that face little public opposition.

Unfortunately, unpredictable delays are difficult to cope with and the increased uncertainty would impact the expected profitability of developments causing, the market to discount the expected value of new developments accordingly. An increase in uncertainty would provide incentives for leaseholders and developers to delay land development until they had more information concerning permissible leases and the plan application/approval procedures had become more established. Since a substantial component of the plan application process involves an increase in a random element of the development approval process, the impact is likely to do more than simply delay the approval process. Related problems will occur as a result of the procedural uncertainty that is inherent in the reform proposals, which award more discretion to the Planning Board, allow public participation, and encourage planner involvement in the plan making and plan application process.

Another type of uncertainty is somewhat more abstract and more difficult to estimate. With a new planning and regulatory system, *informal procedures* will also change. In addition to changing the procedures for approving and implementing plans, the process of negotiating with private developers and interpreting the powers of the planning authorities will evolve. Developers will be less likely to commit to new developments unless they receive a clear sign of support from within the government, or from major interests that could delay development. Similarly, since the legal framework for enforcing the new system will be untested, the court system will be responsible for defining its boundaries. For example, the notes attached to OZPs (Section 16) were not given statutory authority until after the *Town Planning Amendment* (1974) was passed allowing these plans to be used as general guidelines for land development. Given the common law framework in which the Hong Kong system has developed, these new procedures will take time to identify.

The third type of uncertainty which will emerge if the new system is adopted is the one likely to have the most important economic impact, though it is also the most difficult to estimate. This is the *philosophical shift* in planning practice that may take place under the new system. Not only is the current system well known, it is also fundamentally non-interventionist in practice. Since the new system is intended to give planners more discretion over development, this implies that less flexibility will be given to developers. To the extent that the new system facilitates more interventionist planning, the current system of property rights will be significantly effected. Thus, those investing in Hong Kong's property market will be unclear about the stability and respect for property rights under the new system. Just as developers bid on leases assuming that they will be able to build to the maximum developable potential of the site, one would expect they would incorporate maximum delays into their calculations until new rules evolve concerning the objection process and more experience is gained with respect to actual (rather than potential) delays in the development process.

In sum, the implementation of the new system would inevitably infuse uncertainty into the existing planning process, and property markets will respond accordingly. The costs are not simply delays that can be anticipated by the private market since there will be significant random elements.

Chapter 6

Costs of Delays in Development

Previous chapters presented the basic features of the proposed changes to Hong Kong's *Town Planning Ordinance*. Centralizing planning and plan enforcement in a Planning Authority will allow planners to exert substantial control over development and land-use. The result, from the perspective of the government and the planners, would be more consistent and harmonious land-use development. There are, however, potentially significant costs associated with changing the current planning system. This chapter will review the nature of these costs and outline the potential impacts on development for Hong Kong.

Costs of Delaying Development

Delays in the plan making process appear to pose few specific problems for the development community or the economy of Hong Kong unless they interfere with the plan application process or contribute to the breakdown of the contractual nature of land development. The proposals allow for more public participation in the development of plans, particularly OZPs, but these changes simply clarify the process by which the rules for future development are determined. This is already done through restrictions placed on leases when they are purchased.

The impact of the proposals will be felt in the plan application process. To the extent that the plan making process includes sites being considered for development, the delays will have clear impacts on the pace and pattern of economic development. If the development includes Column Two uses, the development must be approved by the

Town Planning Board. Since almost all new developments include Column Two uses, the public participation provision of the Town Planning Ordinance has potentially wide-ranging implications for the development community. (The Town Planning Board currently reviews over 300 applications every year.) In addition, if applications are rejected, resources will be expended in appeals and lobbying, increasing the financial burden of the reform on the government as well as on developers.

The nature of the financial burden of the reforms to the planning process will vary depending on market conditions and case load. Most planners believe that the changes proposed in the Consultative Document will have little impact on current development. Most development, they believe, will occur within existing statutory plans, and delays will add one or two months to the time for processing plan applications.

Nevertheless, these short delays could be significant. Based on estimates obtained from the building and construction industry, each month's delay could add at least 1% to the cost of development, reflecting added costs from money that is sitting idle in government hands and the effects of devaluing the investment through inflation. Given this scenario, a two-month delay would add 2% to the costs of construction. To put this in context, the cost of developing a 500,000 square foot Class A office building is about $2.5 billion (see the discussion of costs below). A two-month delay, according to these estimates, would entail an added financial burden of over $50 million. If the plan application including this development were rejected, added time would be required to cover the appeal procedures. But these delays would not differ significantly from those that exist under the current system and could actually be shorter under the revised system. On the other hand, if the project were delayed by nine months (possible under the proposed plan), objections to development could add at least 9%, or $225 million, to the cost of developing a single site. One developer has suggested that the proposed changes might add $500,000 per day to the cost of development with a lease valued at $1.5 billion (Wigan, 1992). Given this information a two-month delay could easily add $30 million to the cost of a project. A nine month delay, in this case, could tack on another $1 billion.

These figures are not unrealistic given the current state of the property market in Hong Kong. In late February 1992, land was auctioned off by the government at over $5 billion dollars for a new commercial and residential development over a two-day period (K. Ho, 1992). One lot, consisting of almost 95,000 square feet of land that would be developed into a 474,000 square foot residential development in Kowloon, sold for $1.19 billion. Another lot that would add another 475,000 square feet of residential floor space in Tai Po sold for $800 million. If the property market remains robust, the values of new leases, particularly on Hong Kong Island, are likely to continue to increase.

Unfortunately, data on the number of objections raised to new plans and on how often statutory plans are revised were not available. As a result, any attempt to estimate the costs of delaying development are speculative. Nevertheless, given the increased planning activity and concern for development, many statutory plans may be under revision at any given time. The recent extension of planning procedures to the New Territories implies that property development outside the major built-up urban areas may be significantly affected by the proposed changes although events in Tsuen Wan, Kwai Chung, and the Mid-levels attest to planning concerns in Kowloon and Hong Kong Island. Moreover, the extensive reclamations that will result from the airport development and implementation of Metroplan will entail the creation and revision of statutory plans. (One source estimates that as much as 40% of future development will be on reclaimed land.)

In fact, delays in the early stages of implementing the new proposals will likely be much greater than the Consultative Document suggests. While the plan allows for a "maximum" of nine months to hear objections and deliberate on proposed objections, the new planning procedures do not take into account outside political influences such as delays induced by judicial challenges to the planning process or politically motivated delays in the planning process as interest groups lobby politicians and other policy-makers. Until firm legal rules are established through the court system, further delays, which would substantially increase uncertainty in property markets seem inevitable.

On some projects, the Town Planning Board may decide to delay its decision to ensure "adequate" time to synthesize all the relevant information (even though the period for presenting objections may have expired). In Australia, for example, planning approval is required by statute within 40 days of the submission of the application. If a development application has not been approved within 40 days, it is considered refused. The deadline is rarely met. "In practice," notes Jamieson Allom, the national president of the Royal Australian Institute of Architects,

> only a minority of development applications are determined within the 40 day period. For the majority of projects that are not, most professional advisors would recommend maintaining dialogue and good relations with council in an endeavour to expedite a decision rather than taking the precipitate action of lodging an appeal to the court. (1991, p. 16)

Since developers are interested in maintaining good working relationships with the local government in order to ensure the completion of future projects, it is likely that they would make an informal practice of tolerating such delays, which would serve to prohibit adequate accountability on the past of the Town Planning Board through the legal system. Surveys conducted by the Royal Australian Institute of Architects and building industry consultants have estimated that "typical" delays in the development process in Australia can vary from 5 months to 9.25 months, depending on the region (Allom, 1991).

Similar delays and attitudes toward maintaining cordial relations with local planning authorities exist in England. In fact, as in other countries, development in England is subject to delays through extensions of deadlines, consultations with planners and government officials, and approval from planning authorities. Since the merits of a development are determined on a case-by-case basis, exercising development control is fundamentally a political decision rather than a technical one, characterized by "a considerable degree of discretion, each case being interpreted in the light of policy, plans and case law" (Thomas, *et al.*, 1983, p. 214). Indeed, an applicant for development "can never know whether planning permission will be granted, or what conditions will be made" (Thomas, *et al.*, 1983, p. 235). To ensure the completion of the project, developers attempt to work with the planning authorities rather than challenge their decisions through an appeal process.

Delays in obtaining planning permission for development can vary significantly within jurisdictions as well, depending on the disposition of the planning authority and the nature of existing formal and informal application rules. In Canada, for example, delays ranged from two months in Montreal to 22 months in cities outside Toronto (Martin, 1977, pp. 55–56).

The incentive to informally tolerate delays will probably be even greater in Hong Kong than in Canada since there is much less developable land in Hong Kong. In principle, the proposals in the Consultative Document extend the period of public consultation from a minimum of three months to a maximum of nine months. Statutory limitations aside, the impact of the proposals will be much greater than current policy makers may anticipate. Under the new system, virtually anyone can object to a planning application or initiate objection procedures in the plan making process, delaying existing projects. These delays can be instigated by political interest groups such as environmental organizations, historical preservationists or even competitors attempting to gain an advantage in the development market place. It would take only one person (or organization) to object to a Column Two use in a new development and delay the planning certificate for at least the statutory nine-month period, depending on the complexity and sophistication of the objection. Thus, many developers feel the delays will be much longer than predicted despite statutory limitations on deliberations.

In estimating the potential impact of the delays on the economy, the expectations of developers and bankers are key determinants. Since the new system is considered a radical departure from existing planning practice, and will require adaptation to a new system as well as the development of new formal and informal rules, participants in the process will naturally make their decisions based on estimated delays and the experiences of other countries. Uncertainties are likely to be magnified in Hong Kong because, unlike countries such as the United States, alternative areas for development are few. One planning system governs the entire territory and the only way developers can find a "more suitable" business climate is by moving to another territory such as China, Singapore, Taiwan or even further.

One way to estimate the potential impact of these delays on the development process is to trace the impacts through particular developments. As mentioned earlier, one of the principal costs that will be incurred through the adoption of the new planning procedures is the delays in processing and approving planning applications. These delays can add significant costs to underwriting commercial and residential development in Hong Kong. An approximation of the general magnitudes involved in this process can be traced through three commercial and three residential hypothetical projects, varying in sizes, in Tables 6.1 and 6.2.

Again, the extent of the delays will be difficult to estimate. Planners and government officials believe that the new system will not result in delays longer than those outlined in the Consultative Document. They believe the extended public notification process is unlikely to lengthen the development process significantly given the relatively docile nature of public participation in Hong Kong politics. Indeed, even environmental interest groups have trouble rallying significant numbers of people to oppose projects they deem hazardous to the environment. Moreover, lengthy delays are likely only if development sites exist within an area subject to draft plans.

On the other hand, OZPs are continually under review and the timing of the gazetting of draft plans is uncertain. In areas subject to political visibility (e.g., reclaimed territory, the Mid-levels or redevelopments in older areas), revisions of plans may be more common. Indeed, planners have shown a willingness to amend the notes to OZPs when they believe the situation warrants it. More important, perhaps, is the open nature of the objection process. Current proposals do not determine which interests have standing in the

Table 6.1: Cost of Delaying Development of Commercial Projects

(Millions HK$)

Bldg. size (sq. ft)	Class	3-Year loan			4-Year loan			Difference		
		9%	10%	11%	9%	10%	11%	9%	10%	11%
250,000	A	1,303	1,339	1,376	1,420	1,473	1,527	117	134	151
	B	842	865	889	918	952	987	76	87	98
500,000	A	2,606	2,678	2,752	2,840	2,946	3,054	235	268	303
	B	1,684	1,731	1,779	1,836	1,904	1,974	152	173	196
1,000,000	A	5,211	5,356	5,503	5,680	5,892	6,109	469	536	605
	B	3,368	3,462	3,557	3,672	3,808	3,949	303	346	391

Source: Interviews with developers and Hong Kong Rating and Valuation Department, *Property Review: 1992* (Hong Kong: Government Printer, 1993).

Note: Calculations based on cost to developer of $4,024 per square foot for Class A Offices, $2,601 per square foot for Class B Office Space, discounted assuming a 30% mark-up for developers. Data based on average 1991 market prices for Class A and Class B office space for Wan Chai/Causeway Bay Districts.

Table 6.2: Cost of Delaying Development of Residential Projects

(HK$ billions)

Project size (sq. ft)	Class	3-Year loan			4-Year loan			Difference		
		9%	10%	11%	9%	10%	11%	9%	10%	11%
1 million	B	2.467	2.536	2.605	2.689	2.789	2.892	222	254	287
	C	2.449	2.312	2.376	2.452	2.543	2.637	202	231	261
	D	2.413	2.480	2.548	2.630	2.728	2.828	217	248	280
5 million	B	12.335	12.678	13.027	13.445	13.946	14.460	1.110	1.268	1.433
	C	11.247	11.560	11.878	12.260	12.716	13.184	1.012	1.156	1.307
	D	12.063	12.398	12.739	13.149	13.638	14.141	1.086	1.240	1.401
10 million	B	24.670	25.356	26.053	26.891	27.891	28.919	2.220	2.536	2.866
	C	22.495	23.119	23.756	24.519	25.431	26.369	2.025	2.312	2.613
	D	24.126	24.797	25.479	26.298	27.276	28.282	2.171	2.480	2.803

Source: Interviews with developers and Hong Kong Rating and Valuation Department, *Property Review: 1992* (Hong Kong: Government Printer, 1993).

Note: Calculations based on cost to developer of $1,905 per square foot for Class B Domestic units, $1,737 per square foot for Class C Residential units, $1,863 per square foot for Class D Residential units, discounted assuming a 25% mark-up for developers. Data based on average 1991 market prices for Class B, C, and D Residential units on Hong Kong Island.

objection process or the types of uses that can be subject to objections. Thus, even just a few people could raise objections that could significantly delay the process. While mass demonstrations against projects may not occur, more narrowly defined special interest groups that are easier to organize will find the system simple to manipulate. All in all, given the nature of the proposed system and the experiences of other countries with more open planning procedures, the actual delays are likely to be longer than those outlined in the Consultative Document.

Commercial development costs were estimated for six hypothetical projects and three building sizes: 250,000; 500,0000 and 1 million square feet.[1] The estimates were based on average prices in 1991 for Class A and B commercial developments in Wan Chai/Causeway Bay since a substantial proportion of existing and future office development is occurring in these two districts. In fact, the Wan Chai District has already experienced substantial commercial office development, averaging 678,132 square feet per year from 1987 to 1991. The Central District, in contrast, averaged 721,199 square feet of development during this period, followed by Tsim Sha Tsui with 524,207 square feet. In 1991 alone, Class A and B units in the Wan Chai/Causeway Bay districts made up 47.7% of the supply of all private office space on Hong Kong Island and 33.3% of the total supply of office space within the territory.

More important, Wan Chai/Causeway Bay will be leading office development on Hong Kong Island and within the territory over the next two years. Hong Kong's Rating and Valuation Department forecasts that 1.6 million square feet will be added in Central and 3.26 million square feet will be added in Wan Chai/Causeway Bay in 1992 and 1993. In other words, over three-quarters of Hong Kong Island's commercial development and almost one fourth of the territory's total

---

1. Figures and date are often reported in both square feet and square meters in reports, studies and documents referring to construction and development. To maintain consistency, this report uses square feet as the standard for calculating costs (1 square meter = 10.764 square feet).

supply of commercial office space will be added in these districts alone.

Clearly, any proposals to change the planning system will have an important impact on these districts. Interviews with development and banking officials suggested that the developer's "mark up" is between 20 and 25%, although this clearly varies with the state of the economy. An estimate of the "developer's cost" was determined by taking the average market price per square foot in the district and subtracting the developer's mark up, conservatively estimated at 30%.

The total cost of developing the project was then estimated according to the length of financing at varying interest rates. Most development loans are for three years. Most developers expect the planning application and construction phase will take two years. The certainty and stability of the development process in Hong Kong has enabled developers to pre-sell office space as much as 12 months before the building is completed, although the following analysis does not reflect these potential off-setting revenues. Since interest rates have varied substantially over the past several years, the analysis uses three interest rates as bench marks.

The economic impacts of the likely delays in the development approval process will manifest themselves in the added time required to complete the project. If the experiences of other countries are any indication, if the current proposals are adopted new developments will conceivably be delayed by as much as a year (although many in the development community believe the delays will be much longer). As can be seen in the estimates presented in Tables 6.1 and 6.2, a one-year delay can add between 12 and 15% to the cost of commercial or residential developments.[2]

For example, under the new system a 500,000 square-foot Class A office building (about the size of Great Eagle Centre) would see

---

2. It is interesting to note that planning delays for new homes constructed in Orange County, California were estimated at about 16% of the total value of the home (Eggers, 1990b).

development costs (excluding developer's mark-up) increase from approximately $2.6 billion at 9% interest to about $2.8 billion. The change in costs that result from delaying development for one year would be about $235 million, or 12% of the original cost of development. If interest rates were to rise to 11%, these costs would increase from about $2.75 billion to $3.05 billion, or an increase of 15% as a result of the one-year delay.

For a one million square foot Class A office building (a little larger than Sun Hung Kai Centre but less than Central Plaza), which is quickly becoming the standard size development in built-up areas, the additional costs could range from $469 million to $605 million, depending on the interest rate. Thus, a one year delay in the building process adds about $500 per square foot for commercial developments.

To place this in context, about 2.2 million square feet of Class A office space were added on Hong Kong Island alone in 1991. Had every project been subject to a one year delay, as they would be under the revised planning application process, developers would have incurred added costs of $1.1 billion. Hong Kong's Rating and Valuation Department forecasts that an additional 3.5 million square feet of office space will be built in 1992, which would result in an added financial burden of $1.75 billion.

A similar analysis was applied to the residential housing market (Table 6.2). Nine hypothetical projects, varying in size from 1 million square feet to 10 million square feet, were analyzed. The larger projects reflect the higher plot ratios permitted for residential development as compared to the allowed ratios for commercial or industrial land. Developer's cost was determined by using a slightly lower mark up (25%) although the costs per square foot are substantially lower than are those for the commercial development, reflecting lower market values per square foot for residential units.

The estimates are based on units of Class B, C, and D flats and values reflect market prices for residential units on Hong Kong Island in 1991. In general, these three classes capture 83.9% of the total supply of housing in Hong Kong in 1991. Class B units alone (varying from about 430 square feet to 752 square feet) constitute 70.7% of the total housing supply in the territory. Forecasts indicate that Class B units will compose about half of the new units supplied in the private housing market in 1992 and 1993. On Hong Kong Island, Class B, C, and D units comprise 72.7% of total housing supply in 1991. Table 6.2 illustrates the potential economic impacts of a one-year delay in the development process. For a Class B development consisting of 5 million square feet, the total estimated cost of developing the housing estate would increase from $12.34 billion to $13.45 billion at 9%. These delays amount to about $1.11 billion, or 12% of the total cost of development. At 11% interest, costs increase $1.43 billion from $13.08 billion to $14.46 billion, or 15% of the total cost of development. Overall, the costs of delaying residential development amount to about $250 per square foot.

Unfortunately, statistics on square feet of residential units constructed are not tabulated by the Hong Kong Rating and Valuation Department. Nevertheless, in 1991, 3,400 Class B flats were added on Hong Kong Island. Using the median square footage in this class as an average, we can estimate that about 2 million Class B units were added on Hong Kong Island. Costs of the delays range from $222 per square foot at 9% interest to $287 per square foot at 11% interest. Using $254 per square foot (the cost calculated at a 10% interest rate), as a rough guide and assuming that all these units were subject to a delay of one year, the costs to developers would have amounted to $508 million.

In another case, 360 Class D units were constructed in the Mid-levels in 1991. Using the median size of flats in the class, which is about 1,400 square feet, it can be estimated that the total square footage of Class D flats added to the Mid-levels was approximately 504,000. The total cost of delaying these projects would have amounted to $127 million at 10% interest rate.

These estimates, of course, assume that the proposed projects are approved by the Town Planning Board. If the planning commission decided to prevent some of these developments from occurring, or required substantial alterations to the submitted plans, the costs would be even higher as developers scrambled to reassemble a development package more palatable to the Town Planning Board. Some of these costs would eventually be passed onto consumers through higher prices. In addition, small firms would be at a significant disadvantage since they typically do not have resources to pursue lengthy appeal processes or significantly modify plan applications.

On the other hand, the developments may be delayed by the minimum length of time: three months. In this case, the costs would be substantially lower.

Numerous other factors might also impinge on the usefulness of these estimates of the potential impact of the proposed changes. The economic impacts of these changes would also depend on trends in interest rates in Hong Kong and abroad. In the case of residential units, for example, the estimated cost of delaying construction one year increased from $254 at a 9% interest rate to almost $300 per square foot at 11%. For commercial development, costs per square foot increased from $469 per square foot at 9% interest to $605 at 11%.

But, if delays in development become more likely, interest rates will increase. To compensate for the risks associated with longer loans and problematic development costs, banks will extend longer-term loans at higher interest rates. Thus, the previous exercise estimated the costs of delays using a constant interest rate: only the maturity varied. A more likely scenario includes a simultaneous increase in the length of loans and interest rates, even if inflation remains stable. Thus, a 500,000 square foot project that would have cost about $2.606 billion for a 3 year loan at 9% interest will actually cost $2.946 billion since the loan would extend over four years and interest rates would be higher. The added cost for the project would be $340 million, or 16.9% of the total cost of development.

Impact on the Building Cycle

One potentially significant impact of the new planning procedures, if they are adopted, will be on the building cycle in Hong Kong. Although the precise effects cannot be estimated, it is likely that the higher risks associated with the new planning system will substantially increase the variability of the current building cycle, resulting in significant swings in the prices of new commercial and residential units. In principle, if property markets adjusted perfectly and responded to changes in the demand for new units, the supply of new commercial and residential units would increase instantaneously as demand outstripped supply and prices rose. Increasing prices would be interpreted as evidence of strong demand for new units, encouraging investment in land developments.

Yet, new units cannot be supplied instantaneously, producing a building cycle where property developers continually attempt to "catch up" to changing demand for new units. New residential or commercial units typically require up to two years to develop, requiring property developers to make decisions based on their interpretations of changes in demand and expectations about market conditions. Their inability to accurately predict movements in price creates lags in their ability to match changes in the demand for new units with a perfectly offsetting supply, providing the basis for a building cycle.

The introduction of the new planning system would likely exaggerate this cycle by lengthening the supply lag for new units. As mentioned earlier, the new planning process would necessarily lengthen the process for obtaining planning permission for new developments and redevelopments, particularly if they occur in areas subject to new OZPs or revisions to existing plans. These delays could vary from three months to one year or longer, significantly compromising the ability of property markets to respond quickly and efficiently to shifts in demand, and causing greater variations in prices and leases for existing property.

The cyclical effects of the proposed changes would likely be further magnified by the nature of these changes. As mentioned earlier, the length and timing of the delays would be difficult to predict by property developers. Most would consider the delays as a random (or stochastic) factor in the development process. Randomness in planning delays would necessarily increase the uncertainty surrounding development and alter expectations about the state of the economy and the potential profitability of sites. In essence, the uncertainties surrounding development and the delays in the plan application and approval process would encourage developers to wait for more information before committing to significant investments, increasing the lag in new investment.

These effects are well known within macroeconomic analysis (Cukierman, 1980; Bernanke, 1983) and are increasingly acknowledged as an important element of land development. A comparison of planning systems in England and the Netherlands, for example, found that uncertainty with respect to planning procedures and the intentions of planning authorities were important factors in the pace and pattern of development (Thomas, *et al.*, 1983, pp. 245–47). More importantly, to the extent that planning procedures infuse a random element into the process, development may be slowed. "It is not simply the expected length of the delay in considering development proposals which is important," observe economists Stephen Mayo and Stephen Sheppard. "The variance of the delays which might be imposed is critical. Any increase in this variance will adversely affect the current supply of housing." (1991, p. 20) Thus, although the actual effects of the delays are difficult to estimate, the proposed reforms would have potentially significant impacts on the building cycle that should not be ignored. The impact on development will result from both the delay in the point of commitment in the land development process as well as a perceived increase in the randomness surrounding the approval process. These impacts are inherent in the current reforms proposed in the Consultative Document.

Distributional Impacts

If it is implemented, the new planning system will have a disproportionate impact on development. The proposals' biggest impact will be on property rights in the areas governed by older leases: Hong Kong Island and old Kowloon. A property market boom in Hong Kong during the 1970s and early 1980s (before the world-wide recession) stimulated substantial redevelopment in these areas. In 1981, 38% of the usable floor area in new residential buildings in the territory was on Hong Kong Island (Fig. 6.1). Combined with development in Kowloon, over half the new floor area in Hong Kong was added in places with a higher percentage of less restrictive leases. Yet, by the

Figure 6.1: Usable Floor Area of New Residential Buildings by
Region, 1981 and 1990

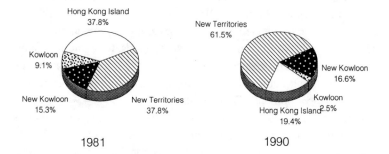

Source: Hong Kong Census and Statistics Department.

end of the decade, most of the growth in new floor area shifted to the
New Territories. In 1990, for example, 61% of the new floor area was
added in the New Territories while Hong Kong Island's share had
dropped to only 19%.

Nevertheless, commercial development maintains a strong
foothold on Hong Kong Island (Fig. 6.2); 37% of all the new non-
residential floor area in Hong Kong in 1990 was added on Hong Kong
Island compared to only 18% in 1981. Furthermore, the share of
non-residential floor area added in the New Territories dropped from
half of the new floor area in 1981 to 35% in 1990.

Thus, planning requirements that place restrictions on development outside the leasehold system would most likely impact the
non-residential property market on Hong Kong Island.

Impact on Developer Confidence

How the market would react to these new uncertainties is difficult
to estimate or project. Accurate predictions of macroeconomic performance are illusive. Some observers argue that the market
would simply make a one-time adjustment as the new system were
implemented: property markets would discount the market value of

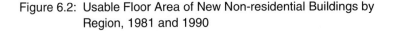

Figure 6.2: Usable Floor Area of New Non-residential Buildings by Region, 1981 and 1990

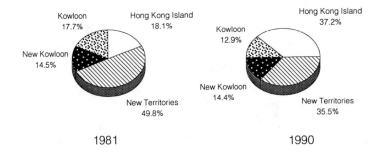

Source: Hong Kong Census and Statistics Department.

properties according to expectations about delays in the development process. In this case, property values might tumble by as much as 20% as developers project the worst-case scenario into their calculations.

More important, perhaps, would be the impact on investor confidence. The planning process would necessarily disrupt the land development process. Unfortunately, as the previous section demonstrated, estimating the magnitudes of the effects is problematic since little data exists measuring the impact of internal shocks on economic growth and development. On the other hand, Hong Kong has been adapting to external shocks to its economy since it first became a British colony. Shocks have included events as wide ranging as the massive immigration from China in the 1950s, the world recession of the early 1980s, and Tiananmen Square in 1989. Recently, the Department of Surveying at the University of Hong Kong estimated that the events surrounding Tiananmen Square reduced the total value of property by 18%, or $285 billion (Walker, *et al.*, 1990. p. 61). Thus, external political events have had important impacts on confidence in the Hong Kong economy. These political events have introduced uncertainty as investors question China's commitment to the Basic Law and property rights in Hong Kong.

Figure 6.3: Completed New Buildings Certified for Occupation, 1981–90

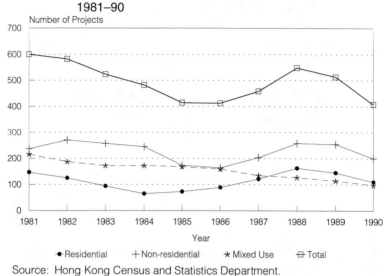

Source: Hong Kong Census and Statistics Department.

Figure 6.4: Construction Costs for Completed New Buildings Certified for Occupation, 1981–90

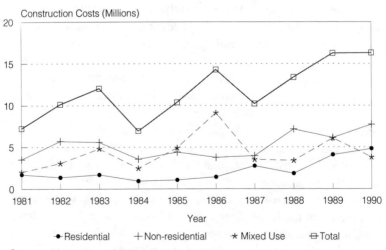

Source: Hong Kong Census and Statistics Department.

While data on the Hong Kong economy is somewhat limited, Figure 2.1 illustrated general trends in real GDP since 1973. Despite world recessions in 1973–74 and 1982–84, GDP increased steadily through the 1990s. Overall, the trend line is consistently upward.

More important for this study, however, is the impact on land development. GDP measures the value of goods and services produced domestically, not necessarily the performance of the economy. A more provocative illustration of how Hong Kong's property market has responded to recent events can be found in Figures 6.3 and 6.4. The number of new buildings certified for occupation decreased steadily from 1981 to 1986, picked up in 1987 and 1988, and then dropped significantly in 1989 and 1990. Dips in building certification occurred after major external shocks to the Hong Kong economy: the world-wide recession in the early 1980s, the negotiations between Britain and China over Hong Kong's future in 1984–85, and Tiananmen Square in 1989.

Construction costs varied significantly during these periods as well. The value of construction declined significantly in 1984, rose to almost $15 billion in 1986, dropped in 1987 (the year of the stock market crash), and then increased until 1989 and leveled off in 1990. Changes in total construction costs seem to parallel changes in commercial and mixed commercial-residential buildings more closely than residential only construction.

This volatility in the non-residential property market appears to mirror changes in prices (Figs. 6.5 and 6.6). Price indices calculated by the Hong Kong Government's Rating and Valuation Department reveal that changes in prices of commercial property varies more significantly than either those of factories or residential (domestic) units. This follows from the volatility of the property markets evident in the number of projects completed as well as the value of construction on buildings completed. The ability of residential units to maintain more consistent prices suggests that demand for residential units may be more stable than is demand for commercial or industrial properties.

What is even more important to note is that these data demonstrate the degree to which the Hong Kong economy is vulnerable to uncertainty. Indeed, despite a tendency to look at the current boom in property values, supply responds to shifts in demand for Hong Kong products and the property markets reflects these shifts. Increasingly, Hong Kong's economy is dependent on service related industries, particularly finance, banking and real estate. These industries also tend to be cyclically sensitive, suggesting that Hong Kong's economy will be even more sensitive to potential shocks, external and internal.

Since the supply of office, residential and industrial property follows changes in market conditions, investment opportunities will change with the market. To the extent that the new proposals for the planning process disrupt property markets or distort market signals, profit opportunities will also be influenced. Thus, as prices fall in the market, developers will still have to carry the costs of construction and of financing the purchase of land for development.

To the extent that uncertainty and development delays disrupt the property boom and prices begin to fall, profit margins will also be squeezed. The developer mark up used in the previous section to estimate the financial burden of delays will shrink even further. In

Figure 6.5: Price Indices for Offices, Flatted Factories and Private Domestic Units

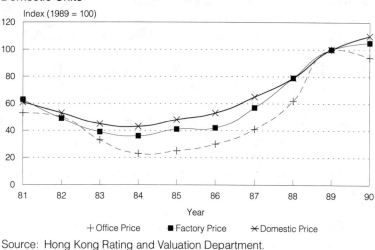

Source: Hong Kong Rating and Valuation Department.

economic terms, the opportunity costs of remaining in the Hong Kong property market will increase, providing incentives to invest in other markets (e.g., Singapore or Shenzhen) or diversify holdings in other industries. The result will be a reduction in the amount of investment in Hong Kong property markets, restricting the supply of new residential and commercial units and putting upward pressure on prices once again. Unfortunately, the risks and uncertainties evident in the plan approval process will hamper the private market's ability to respond to the price increases. Again, as mentioned in previous sections, these economic impacts are likely to be exacerbated because the nature of the changes introduced in the new proposals increase the randomness associated with any delays.

Impact on Government Revenues

While much of the current discussion centres on the impact on developers, the government will also be affected significantly by any disruption of property markets. Revenues from land transactions,

Figure 6.6: Rental Price Indices for Offices, Factories and Private Domestic Units

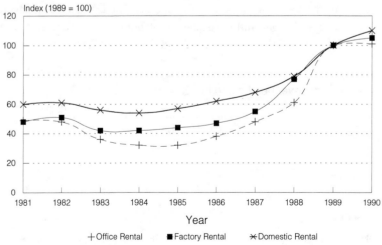

Source: Hong Kong Rating and Valuation Department.

which consist mainly of land premiums, have varied significantly over the years depending on the state of the market and the government's willingness to auction land. In 1981/82, for example, land transactions contributed over 26% of the government's operating revenues, but this proportion fell to only 9% in 1989 and to less than 5% in 1990. Nevertheless, the Hong Kong government received over $4 billion in revenues from land sales in 1990. Although annual government revenues from land transactions vary considerably, and the uses of these revenues is restricted through the Joint Declaration, any significant disruption of the property market will also negatively impact government revenues and, to some extent, expenditures. Any disruption that weakens developer confidence in Hong Kong's property market may also significantly impact the price of leases at public auction, enhancing the fiscal impact of planning policy on public finance.

These impacts can be illustrated through an analysis of the revenue affects which delays in the development process will have on particular projects. Rates, for example, are taxes on occupants and cover all property in Hong Kong unless exempted by the government. The occupier is charged by the square footage occupied. The value at which the rates are assessed is set by the government at $28 per square foot. The revenues paid to the government represent 5.5% of the value of the square footage occupied. Thus, the delayed occupancy of a one million square foot building would result in a revenue loss of $18.5 million for the government (Table 6.3).

Table 6.3: Revenues Lost to the Government: Rates

			(Millions HK$)
Bldg. size (sq. ft.)	Value of property		Lost rates
	per month	per year	
500,000	14	168	9.24
1 million	28	336	18.48
1.4 million	39.2	470.4	25.8

Note: Calculations based on revenues of $28 per square foot and general rates of 5.5%.

To place this in context, if construction of all Class A office buildings on Hong Kong Island were delayed by one year, the revenues lost to the government from uncollected rates would be over $40 million. If the construction of all 3 million square feet of Class A office space in the territory were delayed, the losses would amount to over $55 million. While the amount of office space that would be subject to these delays is difficult to estimate, revenue losses to the government from the general rates could quickly become sizeable if only one or two major development projects were delayed significantly.

Property tax losses are another consideration. The property tax in Hong Kong operates more like an income tax since it is applied to the owner of property (not corporations or firms) and consists of a fixed rate (15%) charged on the actual rental income received. The government allows for a deduction of 20% from gross rent to cover the expenses of administering and maintaining the property. Thus, if a property owner received $25,000 per month in rent for a flat, the taxable income from the property would be $20,000. The tax would be $3,000 per month ($20,000 x 0.15), or $36,000 per year. Thus, an individual owner of 50 flats would normally pay the government $1.8 million in property taxes. To the extent that units are prevented from coming on-line through the planning process, these revenues (like the rates calculated above) are lost forever. Unfortunately, data detailing the number of flats generating rental income are unavailable.

The potential revenue effects of delays in development on the profits tax and stamp duties are detailed in Table 6.4. Two projects were used for calculating the estimates based on data obtained for two recently built commercial/residential plazas. The first project, Plaza A, consists of almost 800,000 square feet of residential and commercial property. For the purposes of these estimates, about 85% of the area will be sold as residential flats and the remaining area will be retained for lease for commercial use. In Plaza B, less than half (43%) of the square footage will be sold for the construction of private flats while the remainder is retained for its rental income.

For Plaza A, sales of flats would generate almost $2.4 billion in revenues. Assuming a 25% profit (slightly lower than in the earlier

Table 6.4: Effect of Delays on Government Revenues: Profits Tax and Stamp Duties

	Plaza A	Plaza B
Sales (Non-reccurring profits)		
No. of flats	1,152	480
Square feet	755,097	298,880
$/Square foot	3,150	3,200
Total sales	2,378,000,000	956,400,000
Profits	594,600,000	239,100,000
Profits tax (16.5%)	98,000,000	39,500,000
Lost interest on 1 year:		
9%	8,800,000	3,600,000
10%	9,800,000	3,900,000
11%	10,800,000	4,300,000
Stamp duty (2.75%)	65,411,500	26,301,000
Lost interest on 1 year:		
9%	5,887,000	2,367,000
10%	6,541,000	2,630,000
11%	7,195,000	2,893,000
Rents (reccurring profits)		
Square feet	120,000	390,000
Rents per month	3,200,000	6,200,000
Rents per year	38,000,000	74,400,000
Profits tax (16.5%)	6,369,000	12,276,000
Lost interest on 1 year:		
9%	573,000	1,105,000
10%	637,000	1,228,000
11%	701,000	1,350,000
Revenue losses from delay:	10.3–18.7 million	7.1–8.5 million

example), profits would amount to $595 million, generating $98 million in revenues through the profits tax. Since delays in the construction of the plaza would merely delay the timing of the sales of units, the loss to the government is merely the interest it would have earned on the profits generated. Depending on the interest rate, government revenue losses could range from $8.8 to $10.8 million on this project.

The government, however, also levies a stamp duty on the sales of flats. While the tax is calculated according to a sliding scale (from $20 up to 2.75% of the sales price), the calculations for Plaza A and Plaza B were made based on 2.75% of total sales. Thus, the delay in construction would also delay potential revenues, amounting to a cost to the government of $5.9 to $7.2 million in lost interest.

The government, of course, also levies a profit tax on the revenues earned through rent and lease (recurring profits). Since, based on the prices and square footage detailed in the scenario, the remaining flats would generate about $38 million in rents for Plaza A, the potential profits amount to almost $6.4 million. The losses to the government as a result of the one year delay would amount to between $573,000 and $701,000.

Overall, the government's loss in revenues on Plaza A could total $10.3 to $18.7 million on this project alone. The losses on Plaza B could add another $7.1 to $8.5 million. While it is difficult to extrapolate to the entire territory, the potential revenue losses to the government could easily amount to billions of dollars as a result of delays in the planning process.

Summary of Costs from Delay

Clearly, the costs of delay through the adoption of the new planning system could be significant. While precise estimates are difficult to calculate, delays could add billions of dollars to current development costs. These costs could be compounded by lags created in the supply of residential and commercial property. In an environment where rising housing costs are pressuring politicians to find relief for the "sandwich class", delays will only exacerbate inflationary pressures in property markets. Lower tax revenues could also compromise the government's infrastructure programmes such as PADS.

CHAPTER 7

Compensation, Betterment, and the Regulatory Impact of Planning Decisions

Town planning and zoning may have the most significant impact on economic growth through its regulatory powers. Government can dramatically impact the economic viability of resources through its power to regulate uses and applications. Planning rules can have pervasive and disruptive impacts on the pace and pattern of urban development by restricting the form, type, and functions of land and property. If a planning board wants to preserve open space, for example, it may prohibit any type of development, effectively forcing the value of the land to zero.

Clearly, the regulatory impacts of planning rules have important implications for property rights and land development. Developers and land owners determine whether they will sell, purchase, or hold economic assets based on their expected market valuations. To the extent regulation alters the relative price of economic resources, decisions concerning their development will be effected.

An important institutional feature of the Hong Kong planning system (as well as of most other planning systems) is the legal exemption from compensating property owners for the devaluation of their assets resulting from planning decisions. This creates uncertainty in property markets since property owners cannot predict with precision the regulatory actions of local planners. To the extent that planners and other public officials become more activist and interventionist, wielding the regulatory powers of the planning system with less impunity, property markets and land developers will be less willing to invest their assets. Indeed, a greater willingness to use the regulatory powers of government will be perceived along with the further destabilization of property rights, weakening the institutional framework necessary for sustaining and encouraging economic growth and development.

Historically, the property development system in Hong Kong has been characterized by stability and respect for the property rights of developers. Indeed, the informal and formal rules discussed in Chapter 5 were essential in establishing the contractual nature of development that acts as the foundation for property development in Hong Kong. Thus, any sign of weakening in this contractual framework will be interpreted as a move away from the implicit commitment by the government to protect private property rights.

Compensation and Property Development

The heart of the debate over economic regulation in property markets and land development is the issue of compensation and betterment. It is interesting that these issues were not addressed thoroughly in the Consultative Document, revealing perhaps the importance town planners place on the economic consequences of regulation. Instead, the issues were relegated to a Special Committee on Compensation and Betterment which released its recommendations in March 1992.

The Special Committee recommended that the government compensate landowners for adverse planning decisions if these decisions deprived developers of "reasonably" beneficial use. However, the special committee represented a legal perspective on the status of compensation and betterment in other countries and its applicability in Hong Kong. The economic ramifications of compensation were not a major focus of the analysis or of the committee's deliberations.

The issue of compensation lies at the centre of economic development in Hong Kong because of the peculiar nature of property development under the leasehold system. When leases are sold at auction, or the government requires payment of land premiums for redeveloping land, land values are calculated based on expected market conditions and assume that land can be developed to the maximum level permissible under existing OZPs and DPAs. By specifying lease conditions and auctioning off property, the government has transferred a development right to leaseholders that can be used until the expiration of the lease.

If the owner of the lease wants to modify the lease to allow for more intensive development, he (or she) must pay the government a premium that reflects the potential value of land at the more intensive use. Historically, the "point of commitment" for development occurred at the time of the sale. This system has provided a tremendous amount of certainty in an economy subject to extreme uncertainty given its political geography.

Unfortunately, the contractual nature of land development in Hong Kong is currently being weakened, as previous chapters have discussed, by a more activist approach to town planning. As mentioned earlier (in Chapter 5), the government is only legally required to pay compensation if land is "resumed" under the *Crown Lands Resumption Ordinance*. The *Town Planning Ordinance* states unequivocally that the government is not required to pay compensation when the value of land is diminished as a result of planning decisions. But many developers see the compensation issue as central to the problem of government accountability and its willingness to use the discretionary regulatory authority outlined in the *Town Planning Ordinance*.

Moreover, the economic impact of weakening property rights can be significant. As planners and the planning authority use their powers to restrict development, the expected values from development will fall, lowering lease prices. This will be particularly important if the government continues to sell leases under one set of conditions only to be altered (often reducing the value of the lease) by another division of the government. These impacts may be mitigated by the allowance of grace periods (as in the Mid-levels). But, as the case of Tsuen Wan suggests, grace periods are not a consistent part of government policy.

Planning Regulation as Taxation

The importance of regulation as a form of taxation is increasingly being recognized, particularly within the economics profession.[1] Few people, however, have extended the analysis to policy impacts on urban development despite evidence of a substantial regulatory presence by the government in property markets. Indeed, the extensive regulation of land development through planning, zoning, and development controls suggests that the regulatory burden may be significant.

The relationship between regulation and urban development may be even more important because of the potential impacts on the institutional framework necessary for encouraging economic growth. While the purpose of government intervention in economic markets is to induce behaviour that would not occur in its absence, the burdens of regulation on particular parties can be significant. Increasingly, these burdens are acknowledged as an important cost of operating in a controlled environment. But, if government intervention becomes too intrusive, development will be discouraged or even halted by the regulatory process.

In principle, governments are faced with two ways of providing public goods (or minimizing externalities): direct subsidies through expenditures and taxation or indirect subsidies through regulation. Often, governments will strictly control entry into particular industries in order to ensure that the "proper" level of service is provided by the private sector. Many regulated industries, such as telecommunications, transportation, and utilities, are part of the "infrastructure of economic growth" (Posner, 1971, pp. 39–40). Regulation also serves as an important mechanism for promoting particular goals, such as ensuring access to services (e.g., health care) by a certain class of people (e.g., the poor) or extending services (e.g., utilities, roads) into new areas to promote geographic deconcentration.

The effect of regulation is to use the private sector to extend services below cost to new consumers or areas, requiring some form of

---

1. "One of the purposes of regulation," observes Richard Posner in the seminal article on this issue, "is to perform distributive and allocative chores usually associated with the taxing or financial branch of government." (1971, p. 23)

cross-subsidization within the private sector organization. Ultimately, however, the service is paid for through higher prices on other products.

Similarly, government regulation of land-uses through town planning represents an attempt to induce behaviour contrary to the natural tendencies of the market.[2] For example, the goals of current town planners include reducing population densities and demands on existing infrastructure. Through planning and zoning regulation, the public sector can prohibit access to resources to meet the housing and employment needs of the community by designating land for community purposes, government use, or green space. Alternately, the planners can restrict uses by imposing lower densities, reducing plot ratios, placing height restrictions on new buildings, etc. While the result will be land-use corresponding to the goals of town planners, the costs will be borne by other consumers (residential and commercial) through higher rents and leases as the number of units is reduced or shifted into areas with low demand.

The principle that regulation is a form of taxation has also been extended to planning and land-use issues (Epstein, 1985; 1988; Power, 1991; Singer, 1992). But the implications go beyond the simple use of regulation to alter private behaviour to meet government goals. Like taxation, regulation entails appropriating private property for public purposes. "Regulation and taxation both may be used as instrument of confiscation," notes University of Chicago lawyer Richard Epstein, "because both are the equivalent of the (partial) taking of private property" (1988, p. 182).

This connection is often obscured or overlooked in discussions of the impact of town planning on development. Many public officials and planners have avoided classifying land-use regulation as public expropriation of private property because the implications for public

---

2. This behaviour does not necessarily conform to public interests. In fact, a substantial literature has emerged suggesting that regulation serves the interests of the regulated rather than the public. See Stigler (1971), Tullock (1967), Tollison (1982; 1991).

finance could be significant. Thus, most planning statutes, including Hong Kong's, legally exempt private parties from seeking compensation for the regulatory impacts of land-use regulation. In Hong Kong, this provision of the *Town Planning Ordinance* has had little meaning because of the government's general pro-growth approach to land development. Issues of compensation through regulatory takings were muted or trivial in this economic policy environment.

Recent activism by planners to control or manage Hong Kong's growth, however, has rekindled concern over the power of the government to partially confiscate land through planning regulation. To the extent that existing law allows governments to ignore the regulatory costs imposed by their actions, the system of property rights that has supported and encouraged economic development in Hong Kong will be significantly compromised. The economic losses attributed to land-use regulation are not trivial, as the following section demonstrates.

Economic Costs of Planning Restrictions in Hong Kong

The issue of compensation for adverse planning decisions is a historically contentious one in Hong Kong, but one which has been largely muted in recent history since the government encouraged rapid development. But the stability of the land development system has been compromised, and with the proposals for reform introduced in the Consultative Document, the issue of compensation has emerged as one of the most salient concerns of the development community. Many see the reforms in the planning system as another step in the weakening of property rights and a move away from a market-orientation in land use development. In at least three cases — Kwai Chung, Tsuen Wan, and the Mid-levels — the government has exercised its discretionary power over land-use without heed to the financial and economic burdens that resulted from those decisions.

In the case of the Mid-levels, the government allowed a grace period during which developers could submit building plans and develop land according to the old planning guidelines (at a plot ratio of 8 instead of the newly imposed limit of 5), an implicit acknowledgement of development rights. Most developers were able to submit their building plans and obtain approval for construction within the grace period, making the issue of compensation moot.

The case of Tsuen Wan, however, raises more disturbing issues. The government negotiated land sales and collected premiums on land for redevelopment allowing plot ratios up to 15. Within weeks, the planning department, acting independently of the government's land sales department, reduced the plot ratio to 9.5 (almost a 40% reduction in development potential). Legally, the government cannot be compelled to compensate the landowners even though the negotiations over land premiums occurred at the same time that the planning department was considering the plot ratio reduction.

Indeed, some government officials believe planning changes that affect the market value of property should be evaluated by property developers in the same way developers anticipate changes in the market. Property values rise and fall according to regional and worldwide economic trends, producing uncertainty in the property market. Changes in land-use restrictions should be viewed simply as another element of uncertainty in an uncertain investment climate.

Yet, planning restrictions impose permanent costs on private developers while markets typically rebound after a period of contraction. Thus, planning restrictions constitute a permanent restriction on permissible development. Many developers view the trend toward more liberal use of planning guidelines (in OZPs and DPAs) to restrict development as a breakdown of the contractual nature of development. While the government will require developers to pay land premiums to redevelop land, the government is not required to uphold its side of the implied contract.

The Mid-levels and the Costs of Regulation

Restrictions on land use can be extremely burdensome financially. The case of the Mid-levels is instructive in illustrating the multifaceted issues involved in the debate over compensation and the contractual nature of development in Hong Kong. According to the explanatory statement, notes, and published amendments for the Mid-levels West Outline Zoning Plan, the planning department reduced the plot ratios for residential development from 8 to 5. The OZP covers 235 ha (581 acres) of which 28% is zoned residential, 19.7% of which is government-institutional-community, and 35.9% of which is green belt (mainly hill slopes and steep terrain). Surprisingly, despite the plot ratio restriction, the estimated population for this district remains the same as before the restrictions at 66,000 (up from 42,000 at the 1986 By-census). Beginning in the late 1980s, several developers purchased land with the expectation of building high rise residential units to meet the rising demand for flats in the Mid-levels area.

Planners were worried that more intensive development would overburden the existing (and planned) infrastructure. According to the explanatory statement accompanying the OZP, the road network was adequate although some areas were congested. Thus, the government was initiating "a number of road improvement schemes" to ameliorate these problems. Nevertheless, there was a "practical limit" to the benefits of reducing congestion through road improvements due to "road space limitations set by existing developments and the steep topography of the area". While water supplies, public transportation, and other utilities were more than adequate, the explanatory statement warns that "there are ... forecasted deficiencies in the sewerage system as a result of rapid redevelopment from low-rise residential properties into high-rise apartments in the area." Thus, to prevent the overburdening of the existing infrastructure, plot ratios were reduced from 8 to 5.

This reasoning is consistent with the general policy-making framework of an administrative state and a narrow interpretation of the purpose of planning roles, but ignores several economic issues and impacts. The amendments to the Mid-levels West OZP (7/9/90) indicate that the plot ratios would be restricted for Residential Group B units covering 43.39 ha, or development in 58.1% of the land designated for residential development under current planning guidelines. This land area would support 37,363,997 square feet of residential development under a plot ratio of 8. According to data from the Hong Kong Rating and Valuation Department, residential units on Hong Kong Island sold for approximately $2,000 per square foot. Thus, the total value of the developable land under the old plot ratio was approximately $74.72 billion at 1990 prices. Reducing the plot ratio to 5 would also reduce the amount of developable residential area to 23,352,498 square feet, lowering the market value of the land to $46.7 billion. In other words, cutting the plot ratio from 8 to 5 would reduce the developable residential area by almost 38%, reflecting $28 billion in reduced property values.

Given the magnitude of the potential losses, the government allowed a grace period for property developers before the new plot ratios became effective. Ultimately, issues of compensation became moot as most developers filed their building plans and development applications immediately. Nevertheless, while these estimates may be high (since they presume all land zoned Residential Group B would be developed immediately to the maximum allowable plot ratio), one of Hong Kong's largest developers estimated that if the planners did not allow for the grace period, the firm's losses would have amounted to $14.8 billion.

Clearly, these losses will be reflected in future market prices for land as the government pursues a more discretionary and interventionist planning policy. Moreover, these losses will be magnified if developers believe the government is working at cross-purposes: one branch negotiating the sale of leases without knowledge of another branch's impending restrictions on future development. Inconsistency in government policy will further increase the randomness of the planning process, reducing the value of land in Hong Kong for developers and lowering the overall level of investment by property developers.

Implications for Economic Growth

Clearly, the losses that can occur from land-use regulation can be substantial for property markets. In fact, based on this analysis, the economic burden of losses due to regulatory changes can be substantially higher than the costs associated with delays in the plan application process that result from citizen participation and increased public involvement.

This brief exercise also demonstrates why a solution to the issue of compensation is crucial to maintaining stability in property markets. If planners exercise their authority over land development and impose substantial costs on property developers, property markets will react adversely. This discretion will be interpreted as an erosion of property rights, since developers will be less certain about the potential uses for which their property can be used, and will be subject to the whims of land-use planners. This, in turn, could substantially compromise confidence in Hong Kong property markets.

Compensation is an important element of the land development process since it holds the public sector accountable for the economic impacts of adverse decisions. If the public sector is released from any obligation to calculate the costs of its decisions, public officials and planners will be more inclined to use their regulatory authority to impinge on property markets, redirect investment, and disrupt the development process. In essence, without compensation, an important instrument of political and government accountability would be destroyed in Hong Kong and, if the government exercised its powers to alter land-uses according to planning principles without regard to the resultant economic costs, the certainty and the stability of the local property market may be significantly compromised.

CHAPTER 8

Conclusion

Hong Kong is at a crossroads politically, socially, and economically. As the territory prepares for its political integration with China in 1997, a healthy economy will be a key component of maintaining political and social stability. Policy makers must recognize the key role Hong Kong's system of town planning plays in ensuring the territory's economic vitality. The current system provides mechanisms for minimizing many of the externalities associated with economic growth while also providing certainty in development. Overall, the system allows land markets to function effectively, adapting land-uses to the changing needs of the economy.

Maintaining this fluid and flexible system of land development is even more important given the radical economic transformation Hong Kong is undergoing. Property markets have become a crucial element in the economic equation, as developers rush to meet demand for better quality housing and office space. The Pearl River Delta and Shenzhen are experiencing a significant economic restructuring, as Hong Kong emerges as the administrative and financial capital of the region and industry decentralizes into the Special Economic Zones. Systems of land-use regulation should complement and facilitate these market changes rather than attempt to overcome them. In most countries, most notably the United Kingdom and the United States, attempts to impose a non-market order on development through planning have resulted in significant resource dislocations within urban economies, reducing their flexibility and competitiveness.

Unfortunately, the importance of town planning in encouraging or discouraging economic development is under-appreciated. Indeed, the recent reforms proposed in the *Comprehensive Review of the Town*

Planning Ordinance could significantly compromise the Hong Kong economy's ability to adjust to changing market conditions. Historically, the ability of Hong Kong entrepreneurs to adjust their resources to fit the changing needs of international markets has given them an advantage in the global market place. This is clearly evident in current investment trends in Southern China. But, by insulating property markets from the rigours of competition for new development and forcing developers to respond to the needs of planners rather than consumers, the reforms will constrain the automatic adjustment mechanism that has allowed Hong Kong to achieve startling improvements in its standard of living and quality of life.

Ironically, at a point in history where Hong Kong needs to maintain its flexibility and adaptability, town planners are suggesting changes that will undercut the Hong Kong economy's competitiveness. Frustrated by the inability to control development, an Advisory Group has proposed several changes to the current system of town planning in the *Comprehensive Review* that will enhance the ability of local planners to override market processes in land development. The new proposals call for increasing public participation in the plan making and plan application procedures and tying development controls to plan applications through planning certificates. The public participation component will delay the approval of plan applications by three to nine months, although the experiences of other countries suggests the delays will likely be much longer.

The planning certificate may pose more serious challenges to the efficiency of the planning system. While the planning certificate allows planners to exercise more control over private markets, it achieves this by overriding market induced allocations of land-use based on the price mechanism. This will necessarily compromise the ability of property markets to respond effectively and efficiently to changing consumer preferences through changes in prices. Thus, flexibility will be compromised in order to provide a more efficient mechanism for planners to move toward their proposed end-state.

The experiences of other countries, particularly the United States and England, suggest that more development control will have limited success in improving the general quality of life of Hong Kong residents. In the United States, extensive planning controls have contributed to inflationary pressures in housing markets. Moreover, development plans have been ineffective in guiding property development toward a visionary end-state. In England, attempts to comprehensively plan cities and municipalities have tended to create long delays and a complicated system of negotiation. The system has distorted prices in property markets and discouraged new development, contributing to inflationary pressures. Both planning systems have contributed to politicizing the land development process.

Thus, the potential impacts of changes proposed in the Consultative Document are not trivial. While many believe several benefits will accrue to the territory through their adoption, the impacts of the reforms will reverberate beyond the offices of planners, planning consultants, government officials, and developers. Indeed, the proposed reforms will delay the development process, increase uncertainty in property markets, and significantly disrupt the contractual nature of land development. Given the prominence of the property market in the Hong Kong economy, the impacts could be far-reaching.

Moreover, Hong Kong property markets are extremely sensitive to uncertainties and changes in global economic conditions. Adopting a planning system that incorporates more development control through the planning certificate system will require significant adjustments in attitude and procedure as new development rules need to be developed and the details of the new planning system worked out. Based on the proposals, the new development control system will involve longer lag times in planning approvals and extensive Western-style negotiations between government planners and private developers over new projects.

Many in the private sector (developers in particular) detect a substantive philosophical shift toward more interventionism as the Hong Kong government moves toward a more representative system of government. This intervention has already become evident in the planning process through regulatory changes in the Mid-levels and Tsuen Wan. If planning intervention becomes more common, and crucial issues of compensation are not resolved, the property rights framework that has sustained the Hong Kong economy may be further compromised.

More specifically, the delays in the planning application system can have significant financial impacts, easily mounting billions of dollars for residential and commercial projects. Estimates using case studies suggested that the added costs to new commercial developments from delays could exceed $1 billion, adding about $500 per square foot. For residential developments, costs could also range into the billions of dollars, adding between $250 and $300 per square foot to the cost of development.

More important, the regulatory burden of planning controls could have far greater impacts if the costs of planning changes are not incorporated into public policy. The willingness of the government to impose costs on developers through the regulatory process (e.g., reducing plot ratios) is seen as a serious abridgement of the contractual nature of property development in Hong Kong, further weakening the system of stable property rights. In the Mid-levels, the potential economic impacts of reducing plot ratios exceeded $30 billion, costs far greater than the potential delays inherent in the new procedures proposed in the Consultative Document.

If the current town planning proposals are implemented, the basic framework of property rights that has been the cornerstone of Hong Kong's economic growth may be breached. The impact on the local economy could be considerable given the volatility of the local economy and property markets. The key element appears to be the extent to which the proposals represent a significant shift in beliefs within the government concerning the scope and applicability of planning principles when they are in conflict with the interests of property markets. The disruptive impact in property markets will be exacerbated if the government proceeds with the current proposals without resolving the issue of compensation.

Thus, the following recommendations may help minimize the disruption of property markets and ensure continued growth:

1. *Design a development application process that avoids unnecessary delays*. This can be achieved by designing a plan application system that presumes development is beneficial to the economy

and Hong Kong society by limiting the time the planning board can deliberate on and refuse an application. Rather than introduce a system (e.g., as has been done in Australia or the United Kingdom) where the application is presumed refused if the planning authority does not act on it, Hong Kong should implement a system where the plan application is automatically approved unless the planning board explicitly rejects the application. This would shift the presumption in favour of development and provide incentives for the planning board (and other public officials) to avoid unnecessary delays in processing applications.

2. *Clearly define the scope and interests of objections to planning applications.* The system as it is currently outlined in the Consultative Document is vague and extremely open. Objections should be limited to parties directly affected by the development and limited to a well-defined list of "bad neighbours" identified by the Town Planning Board and Planning Authority. This would substantially reduce the random nature of the uncertainty implied in the proposed reforms.

3. *Limit objections to the plan making process.* Public involvement is most likely to be productive in the early stages of planning. Citizen participation in the plan application process will create costly delays that could be preempted in the plan making stage of developing OZPs and DPAs. This would allow planners to provide more certainty in property markets by maintaining much of the stability in the current plan application process.

4. *Adopt a system of compensation that preserves the contractual nature of property development in Hong Kong.* The success of the Hong Kong system depends on it being a stable, secure one that arises out of evolutionary, rather than radical change. A system of compensation and betterment anchored to a clear recognition of property rights and the economic costs imposed by regulation is an important element of this relationship. Compensating property owners for adverse planning decisions would reinforce property rights and provide a formal mechanism for their protection in the development and planning process.

5. *Subject planning decisions to an economic impact analysis.* While the Consultative Document acknowledges the importance of

environmental impact statements, it overlooks the economic costs that may be imposed by regulation. Many decisions, such as that of reducing plot ratios in areas experiencing high demand, may be too costly to implement given the trade-offs and alternative means for achieving intended goals. This report is, in part, an attempt to subject planning decisions and recommendations to a more rigorous analysis that incorporates economic issues and problems. Such analysis should become a routine element of plan development.

6. *Eliminate (or substantially revise) the planning certificate procedures.* Diversity, flexibility, and adaptability are essential in Hong Kong's economy and will be compromised if the planning certificate is to force developers to conform to narrow planning concerns with respect to design, aesthetics, shape of accommodation, or other subjectively determined criteria. In essence, the planning certificate should be used merely to indicate compliance with the OZP or DPA existing at the time of development. To the extent that the planning certificate is used to delay development, the economic costs will be significant and yet will give rise to few clear benefits.

The Hong Kong model of land-use planning has provided a capable and effective mechanism for promoting economic growth in the territory. It would be unwise to change Hong Kong's system in ways that reduce its flexibility and stability, making it more like the systems currently in place in other industrialized Western nations. Rather, these countries might find it beneficial to adapt their own systems using Hong Kong as a model. In particular, acknowledging the contractual nature of urban development and embracing property markets as an effective mechanism for allocating land to its most productive uses may help provide a better foundation for sustained economic growth than would imposing severe regulatory burdens on developers through the planning process. Ironically, while other planning systems seem to be edging toward more flexibility and market-driven reforms, Hong Kong appears to be moving toward more control and more centralized planning.

References

Agarwala, Ramgopal. *Planning in Developing Countries: Lessons of Experience.* World Bank Staff Working Papers, No. 576. Washington, D.C.: The World Bank, 1983.

Allom, Jamieson. "Delays in Development Approvals Mean Higher Costs." *Australian Property News*, Vol. 3 (October, 1991), p. 16.

Audirac, Ivonne, Anne H. Shermyen and Marc T. Smith. "Ideal Urban Form and Visions of the Good Life: Florida's Growth Management Dilemma." *Journal of the American Planning Association*, Vol. 56, No. 4 (Autumn 1990), pp. 470–82.

Bauer, P. T. *Equality, the Third World and Economic Delusion.* Cambridge, Mass.: Harvard University Press, 1981.

_____. *Reality and Rhetoric: Studies in the Economics of Development.* Cambridge, Mass.: Harvard University Press, 1984.

Bernanke, Ben S. "Irreversibility, Uncertainty, and Cyclical Investment." *Quarterly Journal of Economics*, Vol. 30, No. 1 (February 1983), pp. 85–106.

Blakely, Edward J. and David L. Ames. "Changing Places: American Planning Policy for the 1990s." *Journal of Urban Affairs*, Vol. 14, Nos. 3–4 (1992), pp. 423–46.

Bristow, Roger. *Land-use Planning in Hong Kong: History, Policies and Procedures.* Hong Kong: Oxford University Press, 1984.

_____. *Hong Kong's New Towns: A Selective Review.* Hong Kong: Oxford University Press, 1989.

Buchannan, James M. and W. C. Stubblebine. "Externality." *Economica*, Vol. 29 (November 1962), pp. 371–84.

Chenery, Hollis, Sherman Robinson and Moshe Syrquin. *Industrialization and Growth: A Comparative Study.* New York: Oxford University Press, 1986.

Chisholm, Michael and Philip Kivell. *Inner City Waste Land: An*

Assessment of Government and Market Failure in Land Development. London: Institute for Economic Affairs, 1987.

Coase, Ronald. "The Problem of Social Cost." *Journal of Law and Economics* Vol. 3 (October 1960), pp. 11–33.

Corr, O. Casey. "Seattle in Captivity." *Planning*, Vol. 56, No. 1 (January, 1990), pp. 18–21.

Cukierman, Alex. "The Effects of Uncertainty on Investment Under Risk Neutrality with Endogenous Information." *Journal of Political Economy*, Vol. 88, No. 3 (June 1980), pp. 462–75.

Dahlman, Carl J. "The Problem of Externality," *Journal of Law and Economics*, Vol. 22 (April 1979), pp. 141–62.

Dando, James. "The Variation of Zoning Districts among Cities." Paper prepared for the 1990 Annual Meeting of the Urban Affairs Association, 1990.

Davies, Stephen N. G. "The Changing Nature of Representation in Hong Kong Politics." In *Hong Kong: The Challenge of Transformation*, edited by Kathleen Cheek-Milby and Miron Mushkat. Hong Kong: Centre of Asian Studies, University of Hong Kong, 1989, pp. 36–76.

Deakin, Nicholas. "Vanishing Utopias: Planning and Participation in Twentieth Century Britain." *Regional Studies*, Vol. 19, No. 4 (August 1985), pp. 291–300.

Downs, Anthony. "The Real Problem with Suburban Anti-Growth Policies." *The Brookings Review*, Vol. 6, No. 2 (Spring 1988), pp. 23–29.

Eggers, William D. "Pruning the Plan." *Reason*, Vol. 22, No. 7 (December 1990a), pp. 22–28.

_____. "Land Use Reform Through Performance Zoning." *Policy Insight*, No. 120. Los Angeles, Calif.: Reason Foundation, 1990b.

Epstein, Richard A. *Takings: Private Property and the Power of Eminent Domain*. Cambridge, Mass.: Harvard University Press, 1985.

_____. "Taxation, Regulation, and Confiscation." In *Public Choice and Constitutional Economics*, edited by James D. Gwartney and Richard E. Wagner. Greenwich, Conn.: JAI Press, 1988, pp. 181–205.

Evans, Alan W. "The Determination of the Price of Land." *Urban Studies*, Vol. 20 (1983), pp. 119–29.

_____. "Town Planning and the Supply of Housing." In *The State of the Economy: 1992*, edited by Giles Keating, Peter Warburton, *et al.*. London: Institute for Economic Affairs, 1992, pp. 81–93.

Fainstein, Susan S. "Promoting Economic Development: Urban Planning in the United States and Great Britain." *Journal of the American Planning Association*, Vol. 57, No. 1 (Winter, 1991), pp. 22–33.

Fischel, William A. *The Economics of Zoning Laws: A Property Rights Approach to American Land Use Controls*. Baltimore: Johns Hopkins University Press, 1985.

_____. "What do Economists Know about Growth Controls? A Research Review." In *Understanding Growth Management: Critical Issues and a Research Agenda*, edited by David J. Brower, David R. Godschalk and Douglas R. Porter. Washington, D.C.: The Urban Land Institute, 1989, pp. 59–86.

Fleishmann, Arnold. "Politics, Administration, and Local Land-use Regulation: Analyzing Zoning as a Policy Process." *Public Administration Review*, Vol. 29, No. 4 (July/August 1989), pp. 337–44.

Fulton, William. "Redevelopment on Trial." *Planning*, Vol. 54, No. 10 (October 1988), pp, 6–10.

Gallion, A. B. and S. Eisner. *The Urban Pattern: City Planning and Design*, 5th ed. New York: Van Nostrand Reinhold, 1986.

Garreau, Joel. *Edge City Life on the New Frontier*. New York: Doubleday, 1991.

Gerckens, Laurence Conway. "Historical Development of American City Planning." In *The Practice of Local Government Planning*, edited by Frank S. So, Israel Stollman, Frank Beal and David S. Arnold, pp. 21–57. Washington, D.C.: International City Management Association, Washington, 1979.

Glasson, John. "The Fall and Rise of Regional Planning in the Economically Advanced Nations." *Urban Studies*, Vol. 29, Nos. 3/4 (1992), pp. 505–31.

Golderberger, Paul. "Shaping the Face of New York." In *New York Unbound*, edited by Peter D. Salins. New York: Basil Blackwell, 1988, pp. 127–40.

Gusskind, Robert. "New Jersey Says, 'Enough.'" *Planning*, Vol. 54, No. 6 (June 1988), pp. 24–30.

Haar, Charles M. and Jerold S. Kayden. "Zoning Today: A Time of Reckoning." *Planning*, Vol. 55, No. 6 (June 1989), pp. 20–21.

Hall, Peter. "The Turbulent Eighth Decade: Challenges to American City Planning." *Journal of the American Planning Association*, Vol. 55, No. 3 (Summer 1989), pp. 275–82.

_____. "Three Systems, Three Separate Paths." *Journal of the American Planning Association*, Vol. 57, No. 1 (Winter 1991), pp. 16–20.

Hamilton, Stanley W. and David E. Baxter. "Government Ownership and the Price of Land." In *Public Property*, edited by Lawrence B. Smith and Michael Walker. Vancouver, British Columbia: Fraser Institute, 1977, pp. 75–118.

Hare, Patrick. "A Peter Pan Suburb Grows Up." *Planning*, Vol. 54, No. 2 (February 1988), pp. 24–27.

Harris, Peter. *Hong Kong: A Study in Bureaucracy and Politics*. Hong Kong: Macmillan, 1988.

Hayek, F. A. *Capitalism and the Historians*. Chicago, Ill.: University of Chicago Press, 1954.

_____. "Competition as a Discovery Procedure." In *New Studies in Philosophy, Politics, Economics, and the History of Ideas*. Chicago: University of Chicago Press, 1978.

Healey, Patsy. "The Reorganization of State and Market in Planning." *Urban Studies*, Vol. 29, Nos. 3/4 (1992), pp. 411–34.

Ho, Kenneth. "Developers Join Forces at Auction." *South China Morning Post*, "Property Post", 26 February 1992, p. 1.

Ho, Yin-ping. "Trade and Industry." In *The Other Hong Kong Report 1991*, edited by Sung Yun-wing and Lee Ming-kwan. Hong Kong: The Chinese University Press, 1991, pp. 169–209.

_____. *Trade, Industrial Restructuring and Development in Hong Kong*. Hong Kong: Macmillan, 1992.

Hochman, Harold M. "Clearing the Regulatory Clutter." In *New York*

Unbound: The City and the Politics of the Future, edited by Peter D. Salins. New York: Basil Blackwell, 1988, pp. 93–108.

Hollander, Elizabeth L., Leslie S. Pollock, Jeffrey D. Reckinger and Frank Beal. "General Development Plans." In *The Practice of Local Government Planning*, 2nd ed., edited by Frank S. So and Judith Getzels. Washington, D.C.: International City Management Association, 1988, pp. 60–91.

Hong Kong Government. *Comprehensive Review of the Town Planning Ordinance*. Hong Kong: Government Printer, 1991.

Hong Kong Census and Statistics Department. *Annual Digest of Statistics*, Hong Kong: Government Printer, 1991a.

_____. *Gross Domestic Product: Quarterly Estimates and Revised Annual Estimates*. Hong Kong: Government Printer, 1991b.

Hong Kong Rating and Valuation Department. *Property Review: 1991*. Hong Kong: Government Printer, 1991.

Hong Kong Office of Town Planning. *Town Planning in Hong Kong*. Hong Kong: Government Printer, 1988.

Horsely, Carter B. "Top Planner Hints at Zoning Overhaul." *New York Times*, 19 May 1974, pp. 1, 14.

Houstoun, Lawrence O., Jr. "From Street to Mall and Back Again." *Planning*, Vol. 56, No. 6 (June 1990), pp. 4–10.

Ingram, Gregory K. "Land in Perspective: Its Role in the Structure of Cities." In *World Congress on Land Policy: 1980*, edited by Matthew Cullen and Sharon Woolery. Lexington, Mass.: D.C. Heath and Company/Lexington Books, 1980, pp. 103–18.

Kahn, Vivian. "California's 80-year Romance." *Planning*, Vol. 51, No. 5 (May 1985), pp. 13–15.

Katz, Lawrence and Kenneth Rosen. "The Interjurisdictional Effects of Growth Controls on Housing Prices." *Journal of Law and Economics*, Vol. 30, No. 1 (April 1987), pp. 149–60.

Kelly, Eric Damian. "Zoning." In *The Practice of Local Government Planning*, 2nd ed., edited by Frank S. So and Judith Getzels. Washington, D.C.: International City Management Association, 1988, pp. 251–84.

King, John. "Protecting Industry from Yuppies and Other Invaders." *Planning*, Vol. 54, No. 6 (June 1988), pp. 4–8.

Kingman, Hildy L. "Zoning with Intensity." *Planning*, Vol. 56, No. 10 (October 1990), pp. 18–21.

Knack, Ruth Eckdish. "Rules Made to Be Broken." *Planning*, Vol. 54, No. 11 (November 1988), pp. 16–21.

_____. "Repent Ye Sinners, Repent." *Planning*, Vol. 55, No. 8 (August 1989), pp. 4–13.

Koenig, John. "Down to the Wire in Florida." *Planning*, Vol. 56, No. 10 (October 1990), pp. 4–11.

Kuan, Hsin-chi and Siu-kai Lau. "The Civic Self in a Changing Polity: The Case of Hong Kong." In *Hong Kong: The Challenge of Transformation*, edited by Kathleen Cheek-Milby and Miron Mushkat. Hong Kong: Centre of Asian Studies, University of Hong Kong, 1989, pp. 91–115.

Kwong, Jo Ann. *Market Environmentalism: Lessons for Hong Kong*. Hong Kong: Hong Kong Centre for Economic Research and The Chinese University Press, 1990.

Lal, Deepak. *The Poverty of Development Economics*. Cambridge, Mass.: Harvard University Press, 1985.

Langdon, Philip. "Pumping up Suburban Downtowns." *Planning*, Vol. 56, No. 7 (July 1990), pp. 22–28.

Lam, Kit-chun and Pak-wai Liu. "Labour Shortage in Hong Kong: Causes, Macroeconomic Consequences and Policies." Unpublished Paper, April 1991.

Lau, Siu-kai. *Society and Politics in Hong Kong*. Hong Kong: The Chinese University Press, 1984.

_____. *Public Attitudes Toward Political Parties in Hong Kong*. Occasional Paper, No. 11. Hong Kong: Hong Kong Institute of Asia–Pacific Studies, The Chinese University of Hong Kong, 1992.

Law, Cheung-kwok. "The State of the Economy." In *The Other Hong Kong Report: 1992*, edited by Joseph Y. S. Cheng and Paul C. K. Kwong. Hong Kong: The Chinese University Press, 1992, pp. 149–62.

Lillydahl, Jane H. and Larry D. Singell. "The Effects of Growth Management on the Housing Market: A Review of the Theoretical and Empirical Evidence." *Journal of Urban Affairs*, Vol. 9, No. 1 (1987), pp. 63–77.

Little, Ian M. D. *Economic Development: Theory, Policy and International Relations.* New York: Basic Books, 1982.

Liu, Pak-wai. *Economic Development of the Four Little Dragons: Lessons for LDCs and China.* Occasional Paper, No. 12. Hong Kong: Hong Kong Institute of Asia-Pacific Studies, The Chinese University of Hong Kong, 1992.

Longhini, Gregory. "Ballot Box Zoning." *Planning*, Vol. 51, No. 5 (May 1985), pp. 11–2.

Macleod, Hamish. "My Six Months Walking a Financial Tightrope." *South China Morning Post*, 9 February 1992.

McKay, David H. and Andrew W. Cox. *The Politics of Urban Change*, London: Croom Helm, 1979.

Martin, Larry R. G. "The Impact of Government Policies on the Supply and Price of Land Under Development." In *Public Property*, edited by Lawrence B. Smith and Michael Walker. Vancouver, British Columbia: Fraser Institute, 1977, pp. 41–71.

Mayo, Stephen and Stephen Sheppard. "Housing Supply and the Effects of Stochastic Development Control." *Oberlin College Discussion Paper in Economics*, 20 August 1991.

McMillen, Daniel P. and John F. McDonald. "A Simultaneous Equations Model of Zoning and Land Values." *Regional Science and Urban Economics*, Vol. 22 (1991), pp. 55–72.

Middleton, Michael. *Cities in Transition: The Regeneration of Britain's Inner Cities*, London: Michael Joseph, 1991.

Miners, Norman. "Moves Towards Representative Government 1984–1988. In *Hong Kong: The Challenge of Transformation*, edited by Kathleen Cheek-Milby and Miron Mushkat. Hong Kong: Centre of Asian Studies, University of Hong Kong, 1989, pp. 19–35.

_____. *The Government and Politics of Hong Kong*, 5th ed. Hong Kong: Oxford University Press, 1991.

Mordey, R. A. "The Search for a Flexible Plan: The Evolution of the British Development Plan and its Future Role." In *Contemporary Issues in Town Planning*, edited by K. G. Willis. Brookfield, VT: Gower, 1986, pp. 1–16.

Mosher, Frederick C. *American Public Administration: Past Present, Future.* Tuscaloosa, Ala.: University of Alabama Press, 1990.

Mumford, Lewis. *The City in History*, New York: Harcourte Brace and World, 1961.

Nelson, Robert H. "Zoning Myth and Practice: From Euclid into the Future." In *Zoning and the American Dream: Promises Still to Keep*, edited by Charles A. Haar and Jerald S. Kayden. Chicago, Cal: Planners Press, 1989, pp. 299–318.

Neutze, Max. "The Supply of Land for a Particular Use." *Urban Studies*, Vol. 24 (1987), pp. 379–88.

North, Douglass C. "Institutions, Transactions Costs, and Economic Growth." *Economic Inquiry*, Vol. 25, No. 3 (July 1987), pp. 419–28.

Nowlan, David M. "The Land Market: How It Works." In *Public Property*, edited by Lawrence B. Smith and Michael Walker. Vancouver, British Columbia: Fraser Institute, 1977, pp. 3–37.

Olson, Mancur. *The Rise and Decline of Nations: Economic Growth, Stagflation and Social Rigidities*. New Haven, Conn.: Yale University Press, 1982.

Paul, Ellen Frankel. *Properly Rights and Eminent Domain*. New Brunswick, N.J.: Transaction Books, 1987.

Peiser, Richard. "Who Plans America? Planners or Developers?" *Journal of the American Planning Association*, Vol. 56, No. 4 (Autumn 1990), pp. 496–503.

Pogodzinski, J. M. and Tim R. Sass. "Measuring the Effects of Municipal Zoning Regulations: A Survey." *Urban Studies*, Vol. 28, No. 4 (1991), pp. 597–621.

Popper, Frank J. "Understanding American Land Use Regulation Since 1970: A Revisionist Interpretation." *Journal of the American Planning Association*, Vol. 54, No. 3 (Summer 1988), pp. 291–301.

Posner, Richard. "Taxation by Regulation." *Bell Journal of Economics and Management Science*, Vol. 2, No. 1 (Spring 1971), pp. 22–50.

Power, Garrett. "Multiple Permits, Temporary Takings and Just Compensation." *The Urban Lawer*, Vol. 23, No. 3 (Summer 1991), pp. 449–59.

Pratt, Joanne H. *Legal Barriers to Home-based Work*. NCPA Policy Report, No. 129. Dallas, Tex.: National Center for Policy Analysis, September 1987.

Propst, Luther. "Report of the Subcommittee on Federal Land-Use Law." *The Urban Lawyer*, Vol. 23, No. 4 (Fall 1991), pp. 651–58.

Rabushka, Alvin. *Hong Kong: A Study in Economic Freedom.* Chicago, IL.: University of Chicago Press, 1979.

Rider, Robert. "Decentralizing Land-use Decisions." *Public Administration Review*, Vol. 40 (November/December 1980), pp. 594–602.

Robinson, Carla Jean. "Municipal Approaches to Economic Development: Growth and Distribution Policy. *Journal of the American Planning Association*, Vol. 55, No. 3 (Summer 1989), pp. 283–496.

Rodwin, Lloyd. *Cities and City Planning.* New York: Plenum Press, 1981.

Rosenberg, Nathan and L. E. Birdzell, Jr. *How the West Grew Rich: The Economic Transformation of the Industrial World.* New York: Basic Books, 1986.

Schultz, David A. *Property, Power, and American Democracy.* New Brunswick, N.J.: Transaction Publishers, 1992.

Seigan, Bernard H. *Land Use without Zouing.* Lexington, Mass.: D. C. Heath, 1972.

_____. "Land-use Regulations Should Preserve Only Vital and Pressing Government Interests." In *Private Property Rights, Land-use Policy and Growth Management*, edited by John W. Cooper. Tallahassee, Flor.: Montpelier Books, 1990, pp. 17–37.

Sen, Amartya. *Resources, Values and Development*, Cambridge, Mass.: Harvard University Press, 1984.

Setchell, Charles A. and Dan Marks. "4 Rms Hwy Vu." *Planning*, Vol. 50, No. 9 (September 1984), pp. 21–24.

Siddall, Linda. "The Environment." In *The Other Hong Kong Report 1991*, edited by Sung Yun-wing and Lee Ming-kwan, pp. 403–19. Hong Kong: The Chinese University Press, 1991.

Singer, William B. "The Effects of Lucas v. South Carolina Coastal Council on the Law of Land Use Regulation." *Cities and Villages*, Vol. 30, No. 10 (October 1992), pp. 6–10.

Sowell, Thomas. *The Economics and Politics of Race: An International Perspective.* New York: William Morrow, 1983.

_____. *Compassion Versus Guilt and Other Essays*, New York: William Morrow, 1987.

Starr, Roger. "Easing the Housing Crisis." In *New York Unbound*, edited by Peter D. Salins. New York: Basil Blackwell, 1988, pp. 170–86.

Stigler, George J. "The Theory of Economic Regulation." *Bell Journal of Economics and Management Science*, Vol. 2 (Spring 1971), pp. 3–21.

Stollman, Israel. "The Values of the City Planner." In *The Practice of Local Government Planning*, edited by Frank S. So, Israel Stollman, Frank Beal and David S. Arnold. Washington, D.C.: International City Management Association, 1979, pp. 7–20.

Sung, Yun-wing. "The Re-integration of Southeast China." Paper presented at China's Reforms and Economic Growth Conference, organized by Research School of Pacific Studies, Australian National University, Australia, November 1991a, pp. 11–14.

_____. *The China–Hong Kong Connection: The Key to China's Open-door Policy*, Cambridge: Cambridge University Press, 1991b.

Taylor, Bruce and R. Yin-wang Kwok. "From Export Center to World City: Planning for the Transformation of Hong Kong." *Journal of the American Planning Association*", Vol. 55, No. 3 (Summer 1989), pp. 309–22.

Thomas, David, John Minett, Steve Hopkins, Steve Hamnett, Andreas Faludi, and David Barrel. *Flexibility and Commitment in Planning*, Boston: Martinus Nijhoff publishers, 1983.

Titman, Sheridan. "Urban Land Prices Under Uncertainty." *American Economic Review*, Vol. 75, No. 3 (June 1985), pp. 505–14.

Tollison, Robert. "Rent Seeking: A Survey." *Kyklos*, Vol. 35 (fasc. 4) (1982), pp. 575–602.

_____. "Regulation and Interest Groups." In *Regulation: Economic Theory and History*, edited by Jack High. Ann Arbor, Mich.: University of Michigan Press, 1991, pp. 59–76.

Tullock, G. "The Welfare Costs of Tariffs, Monopolies, and Theft." *Western Economic Journal*, Vol. 5 (June 1967), pp. 224–32.

Walden, Michael L. "Local Barriers to Consumer Choice and

Homeownership." In *In Missing Rungs: Housing and Regulation in North Carolina.* Raleigh, N.C.: John Locke Foundation, 1990, pp. 9–20.

Walker, Anthony, Chau Kwong-wing and Lawrence Lai Wai-chung. *Hong Kong: Property, Construction and the Economy,* 2nd ed. London: Royal Institution of Chartered Surveyors, 1990.

Walker, Anthony and Roger Flanagan. *Property and Construction in Asia Pacific: Hong Kong, Japan, Singapore.* Oxford: BSP Professional Books, 1991.

Webber, Lyall Alexander. "Careful Road to Planning Reform." *South China Morning Post,* 19 February 1991.

Wenban-Smith, A. "The Evolution, Purpose and Performance of the British Planning Experience: A Practioner's View." In *Contemporary Issues in Town Planning,* edited by K. G. Willis. Brookfield, VT: Gower, 1986, pp. 17–30.

"What We are Fighting For." *One Earth,* No. 13 (Winter 1991), pp. 4–8.

Wigan, David. "Industry Blasts Planning Draft." *South China Morning Post,* 29 January 1992

Williams, John. "City Zoning Blueprint Grows More Complex." *Houston Chronicle,* 16 August 1992a, pp. 1C, 3C.

_____. "McGowen Delays Zoning Plan 2 Weeks." *Houston Chronicle,* 25 June 1992b, pp. 1A, 23A.

Willis, Mark A. "New York's Economic Renaissance." *New York Unbound,* edited by Peter D. Salins. New York: Basil Blackwell, 1988, pp. 30–53.

Wiltshaw, D. G. "Land Investment, Planning Permission, and Uncertainty: A State-Preference Analysis." *Environment and Planning,* Vol. 18 (1986), pp. 207–15.

Wong, Richard Y. C. and Samuel R. Staley. "Housing and Land." *The Other Hong Kong Report 1992,* edited by Joseph Y. C. Cheng and Paul C. K. Kwong. Hong Kong: The Chinese University Press, 1992, pp. 309–50.

Yeh, Anthony Gar-on. *Urban Planning Under a Leasehold System.* Hong Kong: Centre of Urban Planning and Environmental Management, University of Hong Kong, 1991.

Index